D0776752

James Naismith

James Naismith

The Man Who Invented Basketball

BY ROB RAINS
WITH HELLEN CARPENTER

Foreword by Roy Williams

TEMPLE UNIVERSITY PRESS
Philadelphia

Temple University Press
1601 North Broad Street
Philadelphia, PA 19122
www.temple.edu/tempress

Copyright © 2009 by Temple University
All rights reserved
Published 2009
Printed in the United States of America

∞ The paper used in this publication meets the requirements of the American
National Standard for Information Sciences—Permanence of Paper for Printed
Library Materials, ANSI Z39.48-1992

Library of Congress Cataloging-in-Publication Data

Rains, Rob.
James Naismith : the man who invented basketball /
Rob Rains with Hellen Carpenter ; foreword by Roy Williams.
p.   cm.
Includes bibliographical references and index.
ISBN 978-1-4399-0133-5 (cloth : alk. paper)
1. Naismith, James, 1861–1939.
2. Basketball—United States—History.
I. Title.
GV884.N34R35 2009
796.323092—dc22
[B]
2009020102

2 4 6 8 9 7 5 3 1

Contents

Photographs follow page 46

Contents

Foreword

Roy Williams

Before I became the basketball coach at the University of Kansas in 1988, my knowledge of James Naismith was pretty limited. I knew he had invented the game of basketball, and I knew he had been the first coach of Kansas, but that was basically the extent of what I knew.

Dean Smith, my coach at North Carolina, had gone to Kansas and played under Phog Allen, who had been a student of Dr. Naismith's. Though Coach Smith told many stories about Dr. Allen, he did not talk much about Naismith—not surprising, considering that Coach Smith did not arrive in Lawrence until several years after Dr. Naismith's death in 1939.

During the 15 years that I lived in Lawrence and coached at Kansas, however, I learned a great deal more about Dr. Naismith, and I developed an appreciation for the full history and tradition of basketball at the university, dating back to Dr. Naismith's time on campus. I really came to admire and respect the legacy that he built, not only at KU but throughout the world.

It's hard to imagine the world of athletics today without the sport of basketball. Dr. Naismith created the game simply to give college students a physical education activity to keep them busy in the winter, and I know he could never have imagined, even in his wildest dreams, what would happen to his sport in the future.

He and Dr. Allen, whom many consider the father of basketball coaching, had many disagreements over the years about the purpose of basketball and the role that a coach should play. Dr. Naismith was not worried about whether his team won or lost a particular game. He even worked as the referee for many of Kansas's games in the early 1900s when he was coaching, and his teams lost several of those contests.

I can assure you that, if I were the referee for my team's games today, we would never lose.

The game today has changed from Dr. Naismith's era, and one of the biggest changes has come in the importance of winning and losing games. There is so much money involved in collegiate basketball today that winning is often viewed as the most important aspect of a program's success. Dr. Naismith would no doubt be upset by that.

There is no question that his values, and the things that he stood for, are exactly what all coaches should strive to achieve in college basketball. We should be concerned with the welfare of the young men we are coaching, and we should realize that playing basketball is only part of their college educational experience and part of their maturing process. I think we coaches tend to lose sight of that at times.

Dr. Naismith did not approve of some of the changes that occurred in the game during his lifetime, and I know if he were alive today there are aspects of the current game he would not like. I think he would be stunned by how physical the play has become, and he would be stunned by the commercialism of the game and the importance of the game. But I also think that he would like the way the college and high school game is played today.

Dr. Naismith cared about his players as people first, as students second, and as athletes third. He put their well-being ahead of all other issues. He valued those young men who had high morals and values, and he viewed success in terms of the impact he had on the lives of those young people—not whether his team won or lost.

I have been privileged to be involved in basketball my entire life. If the game had never been invented, my best guess is that I would have gotten involved in golf instead. I'm definitely happy that Dr. Naismith invented the game, as are millions of people around the world.

This book tells the story of Dr. Naismith's life, including many personal observations that he recorded over the years. It is the story of a man whose contributions to the world were not limited to the invention of basketball. It is the story of a man who lived a remarkable life.

When I was coaching at Kansas, I often jogged through the cemeteries where Dr. Naismith and Dr. Allen are buried. On game days I would jokingly say, as I patted their tombstones, "We sure would appreciate a little help tonight." More often than not, we won the game.

I know that Dr. Naismith is looking down on all of us involved in college basketball today, and I have no doubt that he is smiling, secure in the knowledge of what his game has meant to so many people for so many years.

The greatest enjoyment that Dr. Naismith received from coaching and working with young people came years later, when he ran into those same people and they told him how big an influence he had on their lives. I have been lucky enough to have some similar experiences, and I think I know how Dr. Naismith must have felt. It is the greatest honor a coach can receive, and I thank Dr. Naismith for creating the game that has allowed me the honor of experiencing that feeling.

Introduction

Hellen Naismith Dodd Carpenter

When my grandfather left his uncle's rural Canadian farm to go to college, he had no idea what the future held. He thought he wanted to become a minister, but what was uppermost in his mind was that, whatever he did, he wanted to find a way to help people.

He had no idea he was going to invent the game of basketball. He had no idea even that he was going to go into physical education. He certainly had no idea that the game—intended merely as an activity to fill the winter months between the sports of football and baseball for a rowdy class of 18 students at the YMCA Training School—would become one of the most widely played sports in the world.

And he had no idea that the sport of basketball would become his legacy—and fulfill his personal life goal.

More than 70 years ago, my grandfather recalled the day that his life changed. It wasn't the day he created the 13 rules for the first basketball game. It was the day when, as a student at McGill University in Montreal, he decided to go into the world of physical education instead of the ministry. During a 1932 speech at the Training School, which by then had become the International

YMCA College, he reflected on that moment, which became his epiphany:

> I was lying on the bed on Sunday and thought, "What is this all about? What is life about? What are you going to do? What are you going to be? What motto will you hold up before you?" I put up on the wall, not in writing, but in my mind this thought:
>
> "I want to leave the world a little bit better than I found it."
>
> This is the motto I had then and it is the motto I have today. That has been a mighty fine thing to me.

It was not an easy decision for my grandfather to pursue a career in physical education. In the late 1800s athletics were viewed by many as a tool of the devil. He had to resist objections of family members when he decided not to become a minister. His parents had died when he was a young boy, and he was left in the custody of a bachelor uncle and was raised in part by his older sister.

Years after his sport had become popular around the world, he wrote, "I asked my only sister if she had ever forgiven me for forsaking the ministry. She shook her head and said, 'no, Jim.' On the other hand I received a letter from a former classmate who was moderator of the general assembly in Canada who said, 'You with your athletics have done more for the welfare of humanity than any member of our class.'"

It was largely through his efforts, and the sport of basketball, that the perception of athletics as the devil's work was changed. He marveled at how popular basketball became in churches, and as more and more churches built new gymnasiums, he was amazed and pleased.

His legacy really should be much more than basketball. He was a man of immense integrity, a man who earned a theology degree and a medical degree even though he never held a pastorate or worked as a doctor. He became a military chaplain at the age of 55 because he thought it was his opportunity to use his talents and give back to his adopted country, the United States. He served more than a year in France during World War I. Near the end of the war, in a letter to his wife, Maude, he offered his thoughts on what should be done for the soldiers returning from the war, basically describing a preliminary form of the GI Bill, a piece of legislation that would not be passed by Congress until 26 years later.

He was always interested in the moral and physical development of young men and women, and he opposed those who tried to make a profit out of athletics. It never mattered to him whether the team he was coaching won or lost a game. It was how the team played, and the character of the men involved, that he thought important. In his early years at the University of Kansas, while serving as the basketball coach, he also worked as the referee for many of his team's games. He placed a high value on sportsmanship, and treasured most the men and women who he thought possessed a high degree of character. He opposed segregation and worked hard to make sure African Americans were treated equally with white men and women.

Even though he invented basketball, he thought wrestling was a better form of exercise, and he considered other sports more entertaining to watch. He would rather have spent time instructing a small group of students in fencing than he would watching a basketball game.

What he valued most about basketball, however, was that it required teamwork, cooperation, and the development of a variety of skills. Having been raised in a very poor economic environment, he also appreciated the fact that the game required very little equipment to play. He once wrote:

Basketball is a team game demanding a high degree of accuracy, judgment, individual skill, initiative, self-control and the spirit of cooperation. It demands that each player be skilled in all phases of the game, thus developing all-round rather than highly specialized ability. Since the object of the game is to have the players of one team put the ball into their own basket and to prevent the opponents from putting it in the other basket, it is frequently necessary for one player to pass the ball to another in order to keep possession of it until a favorable opportunity to make a goal occurs.

If one quotation sums up my grandfather's opinion about basketball, and athletics in general, it would be this: "Let us all be able to lose gracefully and to win courteously, to accept criticism as well as praise, and last of all, to appreciate the attitude of the other fellow at all times."

My grandfather never profited from inventing the game; in fact, he never really worried about money. He turned down endorsement offers, and he never sought a patent on the game, which would have earned him millions of dollars in royalties. His satisfaction came from creating the game and from other, more personal sources. "It would be impossible for me to explain my feelings to the great mass of people as they wouldn't understand," he once wrote.

When I left the farm I had a goal in life—the helping of my fellow beings. This goal has never been changed and as I travel over the country I am constantly reminded of the fact that I have at least given something to the people that will be remembered after I leave.

I am sure that no man can derive more satisfaction from money or power than I do from seeing a pair of basketball goals in some out of the way place. Deep in the Wisconsin woods, an old barrel hoop nailed to a tree. High in the Colorado mountains, a pair of crude backstops; halfway across the desert, a crude iron ring fastened to a weather-beaten barn—all are constant reminders that I have at least partially accomplished the objective that I set up.

On Thanksgiving Day 1918, only a couple of weeks after the end of World War I, my grandfather was still working in France.

He wrote a long letter to my grandmother in which he listed all of the things he was most thankful for in his life. He listed his loving wife, Maude, his five children, and the many opportunities he had been given. He wrote that he was "thankful that I have tried to help the people of the world to make it a little better, and that I have tried to love my neighbor as myself." He prayed "for a clear hope in the future that as in the past the good persists and the evil dies out, that all that is good in my life will go on and the evil will radically be deleted."

At the end of the letter he wrote, "I have tried to fill in some of the details of my cause for gratitude. You know what you do when you have filled in the details of a picture, you move back and see the details in harmony. That is what I do now and see my life as one great cause for rejoicing."

When I was a young girl, my mother became ill, and I spent several weeks living with my grandfather shortly after the death of his wife, Maude. My aunt Maude was also living at his house in Lawrence, caring for both of us. I was homesick and would not stop crying. He asked me if I would go to sleep in his trundle bed, and I said yes. He lay down in the big bed, and he held my hand until I went to sleep. The next thing I remember is waking up in the morning with the sun streaming through the windows.

My grandfather was a man who truly was ahead of his time, someone who understood what really mattered in life. His unwritten motto, which he conveyed to his family members and to those around him, was to "do the best you can with what you have" and "to be thankful for what you have."

When he died in 1939, he left five children and his second wife. My mother, Hellen, was the executor of his estate and thus was responsible for all of his personal affairs. Many of his personal papers and memorabilia were stored in five large boxes that she kept in her basement. My mother moved in with my husband Will and me in 1964 and brought the boxes with her.

Even after my mother died in 1980, the boxes remained largely undisturbed in our basement until the spring of 2006, when, at the request of another family member, I began to look through the boxes searching for a particular picture. What I found was an absolute treasure of items that help to capture the life of this remarkable Renaissance man: not only his documentation of the events surrounding his invention of basketball, but many, many other items showing the man I remembered and loved.

Seventy years after his death, the details of my grandfather's life are still vivid. Many of the young men and women who will make millions of dollars playing basketball may not know the name James Naismith or may not be able to correctly answer the question "Who invented basketball?" As long as they are playing the game, and playing it the way he thought it should be played, however, my grandfather would be happy.

He was a humble, simple, hard-working, dedicated, moral, and honest man who loved his family, loved God and his chosen country, and was proud of his accomplishments. He was a man of high character who was not afraid to take a stance on an issue in which he believed strongly, and he never wavered in his convictions.

He was happy and proud that the sport of basketball brought enjoyment to so many, but he was more pleased that the creation of the game kept him from having to report to his boss at the Training School that he had been given an assignment he could not complete.

It was not until he stood on a reviewing stand at the opening of the basketball competition at the 1936 Olympics in Berlin, the first time the sport had been added to the roster of competitions, that he recognized the magnitude of his invention. He wept as the players for 21 countries walked in front of him, lowering their countries' flags in recognition as they passed.

Through his invention of the sport of basketball, and through the other accomplishments in his personal and professional life, James Naismith, my grandfather, more than fulfilled his personal motto and did indeed "leave the world a little better than he found it."

Naismith no doubt did not consider what he had done to be anything special or remarkable. It was simply what he viewed as the proper thing to do, a lesson he had been forced to learn at an even younger age.

Naismith's father, John Naismith, had moved from Scotland to Canada as a 14-year-old boy and lived on his uncle's farm until he was 18. He then apprenticed himself to a carpenter, working for an entire year for $1. Later he became a building contractor, formed a partnership with Robert Young, and in 1858 married Young's sister, Margaret. Her father gave the couple a piece of land about 200 yards from his home, and Naismith built a house on the land.

The Naismiths were not the only Scottish family to settle in that part of Canada. Many others, leaving Scotland to find a new life, had settled in the same area, a rural section along Canada's Mississippi River just west of Ottawa, which had been selected as the Canadian capital only four years before Jim Naismith's birth. The small town of Almonte had been founded by Scottish immigrants in the 1820s, and the more people emigrated from Scotland to the area, the more relatives and friends followed in the years to come. The area provided them all of the natural resources they needed to lead successful lives and pursue the occupations they had enjoyed in their native country. By the mid 1800s more than 90,000 people had emigrated from Scotland to Canada, living mostly in the rural areas, which remained sparsely populated in spite of this influx.

By and large, these people of Scottish ancestry were sincere, religious, and hard-working citizens intent on building a good life for themselves and their families. Like almost all other Europeans who fled their homelands for the "new world" of the United States and Canada, they were seeking a better life. They were clannish people, and when they wrote to friends and relatives about how much they loved their new homeland, relatives and friends decided to come and join them. The established settlers took in the newcomers and cared for them until they could

• • •

Growing Up

L ate into the night, Jim Naismith worked alone in the blacksmith shop. Spending an evening standing by a fire on the side of a frozen river, having only been able to watch as other kids from Bennie's Corners skated and frolicked on the ice, had driven Naismith into action.

The 14-year-old Naismith didn't have a pair of ice skates, and even in 1875 in rural Canada, most youngsters facing that situation would have immediately run home and begged their parents to buy them a new pair of skates.

For many reasons, Naismith was not like most 14-year-olds. Which is why, after watching the other kids skating, he left the pond and looked around the buildings in Bennie's Corners until he found two old worn-out files. He took them into the blacksmith shop and ground them until they were the size he wanted. Next he found two strips of hickory wood and figured out how to attach the files to the wood. He also made leather straps so that he could fasten the boards to the bottoms of his boots.

After many hours of work, all Naismith had to do was sharpen his skates. The next night, when the other kids put on their skates and took to the ice, so did Naismith.

make their own way. The attitude was that there was "always room for one more."

"The people were not stingy but frugal and thrifty," Naismith's daughter Margaret wrote in a family history years later.

> The women spun their own yarn, knitted as many articles of clothing as they could, even weaving their own blankets.
>
> During the long winters, when the temperatures fell lower and lower and the snow piled higher and higher, the families gathered around the stove each with his work. The men were carpenters and cabinet makers as well as farmers. There were tools to be mended or sharpened, harness to be made or mended while the women had their knitting and clothes to make. It took a long time to make a dress in those days. There were many yards of sewing and all to be done by hand.
>
> They had morning and evening prayers and their church was a very real part of their lives. They preserved the Scottish customs and all together were a happy, contented community.

Since the Scottish immigrants were also interested in education, business, and politics, it was not surprising that many of the early Canadian leaders were of Scottish descent, including James McGill, who founded McGill University in Montreal in 1813.

James (Jim) Naismith, the second of three children, was born in his parents' house in Ramsey, Ontario, on November 6, 1861, joining his older sister, Annie. His younger brother, Robert, was born in 1866. James Naismith did not have a middle initial in his name, even though years later many sources would include the letter *A* as his middle initial. When asked, Naismith almost always replied that the *A* stood for "anonymous."

Naismith was very proud of his Scottish heritage, and the traditions and work ethic he learned as a young boy stayed with him the rest of his life.

A few years after Naismith was born, the family moved to nearby Almonte because his father was working in the area, building a series of houses. Nearly every weekend, however, Jim returned to his grandfather Young's farm. Naismith was riding in a buggy with his grandfather, a cabinet maker by trade, when he got another early life lesson.

"He had to make a call on a neighbor and he left me with strict instructions not to touch a little parcel that lay on the seat of the buggy," Naismith recalled years later. "But on investigation I found that it was a plug of chewing tobacco, which I immediately sampled. When grandfather came out, after giving me time to get the benefits of the chew, he found me in a state of collapse. He did not dare to take me home to my mother, so he held me in an upright position until the fresh air brought me to a more or less normal condition."

On another occasion, Naismith was with his grandfather when they went off into a field. Naismith had a small sickle, and his grandfather a scythe, and they worked to trim the fence row. The two were distracted for a while by a squirrel, and Naismith's grandfather taught the boy how to hunt the animal.

"He picked up his scythe, and we walked home," Naismith recalled. "About halfway home, he asked me where my sickle was. I remembered I had left it when I hunted the squirrel. We sat down, and he told me he could not pay me for that week's work as I had lost a tool and it cost money. He gave me plenty of time to think it over, and then he produced it from under his coat."

Naismith trudged toward home an unhappy boy, because he knew at least a dozen places where he could have spent the money he should have earned that day. Before they reached the house, however, his grandfather reached into his pants pocket, pulled out some change, and said, "I'll pay you half of what you earned today." The boy was not quite as disappointed as he had been minutes earlier.

Another temptation came one day when Naismith noticed his grandfather had a stack of new doors ready to be installed in a house that was under construction. Taking a brace and bit, for no real reason, Naismith drilled a perfect hole through the stack of doors. Jim received another scolding that night.

Naismith began school in Almonte, and when he was 7, the family moved to a small village on the Ottawa River called Grand Calumet Island. His father bought a sawmill there to create his own source of lumber, thinking it easier to ship the lumber to the cities than to ship the logs down the river to another sawmill.

Naismith barely avoided a tragedy one day when he was in the mill and the workers were all in another part of the mill. "I took up a cant dog and began to roll the log towards the saw," Naismith wrote years later. "My father, hearing something going on above, rushed upstairs just in time to see an immense log rolling towards his son. Fortunately, I had dropped the cant hook and it caught the log before it had rolled over me."

It wasn't just when he was hanging around the mill that Naismith got himself into trouble. Outside, he often spent time with members of the teamsters who worked in the area. Naismith recalled how they enjoyed giving him an old blackened pipe to smoke. "I was eight years old and I could smoke a pipe with the best of the teamsters," he said.

Naismith wanted to learn to operate the machinery in the mill, and one day he complained to his father that another boy, Johnny Wilson, only slightly older than Naismith, was allowed to work on the machines. The elder Naismith explained to his son that he wanted him to receive an education, so that one day he could help run the business. "This made an impression on me, so that I was willing to forego the saw mill," Naismith said. "This was doubtless helped along when not long after Wilson came to the house minus a thumb."

Naismith thought his future was in place, but his plans began to change in the summer of 1870, when in the space of four months he had to endure the death of his beloved grandfather, the loss of the sawmill, and the deaths of both his mother and father.

Grandfather Young died on July 17 at the age of 68. While the family was still in mourning, the sawmill was destroyed in a fire. While Naismith's father was determining how to recover from that tragedy, he contracted typhoid fever. Epidemics were not uncommon in rural areas in that period, and once someone became ill, there was little the few doctors could do to stop the disease from spreading throughout the family and the community.

The news of John Naismith's illness reached family members in Almonte, and his brother-in-law, William, thought of his sister and the three children. Not listening to the suggestions of his wife that other family members could care for them, William Young harnessed horses to a sleigh and headed for the Naismiths' home.

Arriving there, he told his sister to get the children's clothing and she complied, kissing the three children goodbye and telling them to go off with their uncle. The last vision Naismith had of his mother was of her standing at the doorway to their home, proudly waving goodbye. Naismith's father was too sick to get out of bed, and the children were forbidden to go near him for fear they would catch the disease.

Uncle William and his family did their best to care for the children, but no one could stop the effects of the disease. John Naismith died on October 19. Less than three weeks later, Margaret Naismith also died, having contracted typhoid fever while caring for her sick husband. She died on November 6, which was also Annie's twelfth birthday and Jim's ninth birthday. John and Margaret were both only 37 years old. They were buried quickly in a town near the river island.

The children moved into the home of their grandmother Young and Uncle Peter, a bachelor, halfway between Bennie's Corners and Almonte. There were many days when Jim missed his mother, and he remembered her telling him that when she was a young girl, living in the same house, she would often play in the grain bin. Whenever he thought of his parents and was afraid he could not hold back the tears, he ran to the grain bin and crawled inside, where he "talked" with his mother.

Years later, Naismith's daughter Hellen recalled how much her father missed his parents, despite the best efforts of his grandmother to provide the children with a good life. "She was a wonderful woman and did everything she could for the children, but he never got over wanting his own mother," Hellen Naismith wrote in 1957. "As a consequence of this he put all mothers on a pedestal and to him they were something very special.

"When little boy troubles became pretty heavy and no one seemed to understand he would go to the barn, crawl into the feed box, pull the cover down and talk to his mother. She seemed a little closer there in the dark. When he left the barn, often with a tear-streaked face, he felt the world wasn't such a bad place and that things would be better."

The sadness of missing his mother and father was to stay with Naismith all of his life, and it affected the way he viewed relationships in other families. "No one who has not experienced it can appreciate the longing a boy has for a father or mother," he wrote years later. "It made me furious when my cousins would be discourteous to their parents. I used to think that if they did not have one they would act very different."

On February 3, 1873, Naismith's world changed again when his grandmother died, leaving him, his sister, and his brother in the care of their bachelor uncle, Peter, only 12 years older than Annie. During his grandmother's funeral, Naismith recalled, he and his brother were upstairs in their bedroom, above the kitchen. He pulled out an old fiddle from under the bed and began to play "Home, Sweet Home," "after a fashion." The music carried down the stairs. As more and more of the friends and relatives assembled for the funeral began to turn their heads toward the door, Naismith's Aunt Jeannie slipped out of her seat and went to investigate. She found Naismith and his brother and the other children playing music. She "took the fiddle away from me and broke it across her knee," Naismith said. "Thus all desire for music died in my soul."

The children's uncle was determined to be as good a guardian as possible. He insisted the children go to school, walking the two and a half miles even on the harshest of winter days, when the temperature often plunged to 30 degrees below zero. Naismith and his sister Annie were walking home one day when they noticed that a bear and two cubs had begun to follow them. "My sister, being older than I, could outrun me and she kept turning around and calling out 'run Jim, they are just behind you.' I ran the best I could," Naismith said, "not because I was afraid of what the bear would do to me but I did not want her to chew up my new boots."

The bears finally stopped giving chase, but Naismith recalled the incident a few years later when he once again spotted what he thought was a bear in the moonlight. He picked up a stone and prayed to God to help him: "I marched ahead determined to throw the stone and gave a terrific yell. As I approached the animal I saw that it was a white cow with a great black spot on her side. I breathed a sigh of relief and went on home. I have often wondered if the Lord gave me courage to go ahead and find out that it was really a cow, or if in answer to my prayer, He changed the bear into a cow."

Naismith's life consisted of going to school, working on the farm, and playing a variety of games with his friends. Though he got into many scrapes, he recalled in particular how one big tall boy was constantly taunting him and coaxing him into fights. Six times they fought and Naismith lost, but in their seventh battle Naismith emerged the winner, raising his self-esteem a notch.

Just as grade school in Bennie's Corners was two and a half miles in one direction from the family home, the high school, in Almonte, was the same distance in the opposite direction. Naismith was not the most gifted student, and throughout his school years he was less interested in studying than in being outdoors—whether doing work on his uncle's farm, working in lumber camps, or playing games, swimming, or fishing with his friends. "I put up with the lessons for the sake of the recess and the dinner hour, and what I learned was largely by absorption rather than by hard work," Naismith wrote. "As an illustration one night I was kept in to learn to spell some words and at the same time Peter Young [a cousin] was kept in to learn a piece of poetry. I learned the poetry but do not remember learning to spell the words."

Bobsledding and tobogganing were frequent activities during the winter, along with ice skating, and when the weather was warmer, Naismith and friends could frequently be found swimming or fishing in the Indian River. "It was typical boys' play in the water and they ducked each other and used the mud banks for a slippery slide," Naismith said.

In the fall, the boys hunted birds and rabbits in the field and tried to catch the great northern pike in the river. Naismith was particularly adept at going out in a canoe at night and spearing a fish.

During the evenings, a group of youngsters almost always found themselves hanging around the blacksmith shop in Bennie's Corners, which by the 1870s had lost much of its status as a successful village because of a fire in 1851 that destroyed much of the town. When Naismith was growing up, the area consisted primarily of a few homes, the grade school, a store, and the blacksmith shop. "It was a common sight," he recalled, "to see a group of boys gathered about the anvil in the blacksmith shop trying to out-lift each other. One of their favorite stunts was to try and lift the anvil by grasping the tapering. In the sugar bush back of the shop some of the boys tried to do some stunt that none of the others would dare. They would swing from one branch to another or run along a limb far above the ground, risking arms and legs in an effort to out-do [the] competition."

Most of the contests came about after a spur-of-the-moment suggestion by one of the youngsters. These games, which often featured high jumping, wrestling, or fighting, were created by the kids to give them something to do. Another frequent contest was tug-of-war, but Naismith's favorite game, and the preferred game for many of his friends, was called "Duck on the Rock."

The game combined tag with throwing. The "goal" was a large rock. Each youngster had a small stone, and to start the game one youngster, selected as the "guard," placed his stone on top of the rock. The other youths formed a line about 15 to 20 feet away. For each youngster, the objective was to throw his stone and knock the guard's stone off the rock. If he was successful, he went to the end of the line and waited for his next turn. If he missed, a race was on. If the guard tagged the youth who had thrown the stone before he reached his stone, the two had to trade places. "More often than not, [the boys] missed, and when they went to retrieve the duck, the guard could tag them," Naismith noted in later years. He said he enjoyed the game because it combined alertness, good timing, and dodging ability.

Over time, the youngsters discovered that if the stone was thrown like a baseball, it would bound farther away, increasing the likelihood that it would be recovered by the guard. Throws made with an arc proved to be more accurate and more successful, and even if the shot missed, the stone would not bounce too far away. The game was played at recess and at night, and would become far more important to Naismith in the years to come.

During his teenage years, other than carousing with his friends, Naismith's most common activities were working on the farm and assisting his uncle with the chores. He often missed going to school when there was extra work to be done on the farm, so it was not a total surprise when he announced, during his sophomore year in high school, that he was quitting school to work full-time on the farm.

During the winter, when there was less work to do on the farm, Naismith went to work in the lumber camps, and that experience also had a major influence on his future. "I recall one incident that may have had a lot to do with setting me to thinking,"

Naismith said. "When I was about 14, I was working one day with the farmers as they were repairing the road, working out their poll tax. One of their number passed a black bottle from which many took drinks. On the second round, he insisted that I drink also. At my refusal, my half cousin, Pete Naismith, somewhat tipsy, came over and declared, 'James Naismith can take a drink if he wants to, and he can leave it alone if he wants to. I knew his mother, and I don't think she would want him to drink, and there isn't a man here that can make him if he doesn't want to.'"

Working in the lumber camps exposed Naismith to a social element that he had not previously experienced. He came into contact with people of different backgrounds and different morals, and like anybody else put into that situation, he wanted to fit in and be accepted as one of the group. It was his sister, Annie, who reminded him that his mother would have been upset by the way he was living his life, and Naismith realized his sister was right.

Earlier, Naismith had discovered that his younger brother, Robert, had been given whiskey to drink as part of his diet. "One day it occurred to me that . . . this was a good way to make a drunkard of him," Naismith said. "We talked it over and agreed that we would not touch it again and we kept to our promise."

After the incident with the farmers, Naismith and his brother took a pledge in the church that "as long as my name was on that book I would not drink liquor as a beverage." This pledge was soon tested when Naismith was driving a sled and his path was blocked by men determined to make him drink whiskey. "I reached forward and loosened a sleigh stake and told them that I would brain them if they did not go on about their business," he said. Years later, Naismith claimed that it was those teenage challenges with a bottle of whiskey that "made me measure my conduct in the light of what mother would have wanted me to do."

Naismith's mother likely would have been disappointed by her son's decision to drop out of school, even if he did have his reasons. She would have approved, however, of his work ethic. His uncle Peter gave Naismith a team of horses and put him to work full time in the fields. For some time Naismith had talked about his desire to have his own buggy with red wheels, and now he finally had one.

Naismith received a lesson in self-reliance one day when he got himself and his horses into trouble crossing the Misiwaka River. "I had been sent across the river for a load of hay," he recalled. "The road that we usually used was down the stream, and I was determined to try a new way. I crossed the ice with the sled and put on my load. I had almost crossed on the return trip when with a crash one of the team went through the ice. I had hit a spring hole. The other horse followed and now both were in the water.

"To run for help would have lost the team, and it was up to me to try and get the team to shore. . . . I can well remember the lump that rose in my throat. A valuable team of horses was struggling in the water, simply because I had been in too much of a hurry to go a quarter-mile down the stream. Luckily the sleigh had not gone through the ice and I went around and unfastened the doubletree. Next I took a rein and fastened it around one of the horse's necks as he kicked and thrashed. I worked him up onto the ice again. I repeated my tugging and finally got both horses to the shore.

"This incident was one of many that happens to boys in the country and it is this type of thing that the boy in the city has little opportunity to experience."

As he and the horses recovered on the shore, Naismith happened to glance behind him and saw his Uncle Peter, standing beside a tree. "I never knew how long he had stood there," Naismith said, "but I am sure he was there before I had pulled the horses out." The lesson Naismith learned was that when he got into trouble, he had no one he could rely on to get him out of the mess except himself.

"When a boy was sent with a team into the field he was expected to handle the team and any emergency that might arise," he observed. "Often he would be far from the house and if he broke a single tree snaking out logs it was up to him to fix the part and continue with his work."

In 1876 fate again entered Naismith's life. He had become friends with a nine-year-old boy, Robert Tait McKenzie, the son of the local Presbyterian minister. One Sunday, after preaching his sermon, the Reverend McKenzie died from a heart attack, leaving behind his widow and three young children. The family had to leave the home provided by the church to make way for the new minister, and the community came together to raise money to build the family a new home. While it was under construction, however, the family needed a place to stay, and Tait McKenzie wound up moving in with Naismith, the foundation of a friendship that was to bloom when they were in college and last the rest of their lives.

McKenzie later recalled how he looked up to and admired Naismith. "Jim was the hero of many boyish exploits," McKenzie declared. "Spearing fish on the flooded flats in spring by the light of the jack filled with pine knots; hunting the dogs that killed the sheep; riding, rowing, working and fishing in summer; made the round of life on the farm, with the winters in school at Almonte. His challenge of the wheat sheaf was characteristic of his love of competition."

McKenzie was particularly impressed when Naismith was binding wheat. "In one hand he holds a sheaf he has just bound," McKenzie wrote. "He throws it up in the air, stoops and binds another sheaf before the first one comes back to Earth, and challenges anyone on the harvest field to do the same thing."

While Naismith had a great deal of influence on the younger McKenzie's development, it might have been at least partially due to McKenzie's influence, over a span of a few years, that Naismith made the decision to return to high school. He was 19, an age when most youths had already completed school. If his age did not pose enough of a problem, the school administrators made the unusual decision that Naismith would have to re-enroll as a freshman, beginning classes with youths five years younger.

When he told his uncle of his decision, Naismith finally admitted at least part of the reason why he had dropped out five years earlier. "I told my uncle it was because I was getting in with a crowd of boys that did not think or act as I did and I was afraid that I would become like them," Naismith said. This was no doubt a true statement, but it also was obvious that, at the time he dropped out, Naismith did not see the value of additional education. By the age of 19, his opinion had changed.

For some time, because Naismith "could not make a decent milk stool," his uncle had been encouraging him to make his living with his head and not his hands. "I wanted to show him that I could make something good and I spent the afternoons making a sideboard," Naismith remembered. This effort must not have gone well, because "suddenly it dawned on me that perhaps he was right."

Naismith's life might have turned out differently, however, had the Northwest Mounted Police not told him and his friend that they were too young when they tried to enlist. Naismith's friend did go back in a later year and was allowed to enlist, but by that time, Naismith said, "I had an aim in life."

Naismith's aim was to graduate from high school and go on to college. His first goal was to become a doctor, but he decided that morally he was not equipped for that job. "Some things that a doctor should do I did not feel that I could do, such as letting a badly deformed baby die," he said. Instead, Naismith decided to study for the ministry. He convinced the high school administrators of his seriousness, and halfway through his first year he was allowed to skip a grade. The same thing happened the following year, so it turned out that Naismith needed only two years to complete the four years of study. He often stayed up late at night studying, and he used the time walking to and from school to memorize his assignments.

"Sciences were easy for me but the languages were difficult," he said. "There were 42 in our class in the regular subjects and in math and geometry; I was not far from the head. But in grammar, I was 42nd and if there had been 50 I would have been that number.

"One day the superintendent kept me after school and began to question me. He said, 'Naismith, you do well in most of your subjects but in grammar you are no good. What is the matter?' I told him that I knew all the rules and could repeat them correctly but I did not see any use for them. He went to the blackboard and analyzed a sentence, explaining what he was doing.

"I stopped him and said, 'Is that what you are driving at?' He said that was what he wanted. I told him that was all I needed and soon I was near the head in that class also."

In his senior year, a teacher in a rural school took ill, and Naismith was asked to teach the class for the rest of the term. When an inspector came to check, he found Naismith's students were the lowest in mathematics and the best in grammar. Naismith learned another lesson—that it was often easier to teach a subject you had struggled to learn than one that had come more easily.

Naismith knew he would have to pass exams in Latin and Greek to be admitted to McGill University in Montreal, so he spent all of his spare time studying those subjects. Greek proved to be a particular challenge. "I studied Xenophon's *Anabasis*, spending two weeks on the first sentence," Naismith recounted. "By fall I had covered half of the book, and went up for matriculation examination. When the paper in Greek was opened, I found that at least half of the paper was from that part of the book that I had never touched. But I did the best I could and passed."

Even though admitted to McGill, Naismith had not determined exactly how he was going to pay for college. One day, his uncle came up to him and asked that question. Naismith said he would find a way. "He then told me that if I would come home in the summer [and work on the farm] he would pay my expenses during the winter," Naismith explained. "I gladly jumped at this chance."

In the fall of 1883, Naismith headed off to college.

CHAPTER 2

The College Years

Not only did Naismith have to adjust to college life, but the move from the farm and the rural community of Almonte to the big city of Montreal also required him to adapt to a new environment. "As I walked down the street a peculiar feeling came over me," he wrote later. "I had always lived in a community where everyone knew me and to a great measure controlled my actions. Here I was, in a city, on my own. No one knew me and what I did was my own business. This feeling was indeed new to me and for several days I lived largely in the realization that I was my own boss."

One of the first decisions that Naismith made was that his studies would be his top priority. He was confident that his decision to enter the ministry was the proper one for him, but he had to receive his bachelor's degree before he could qualify for the School of Theology. "I determined to accomplish this as soon as possible and set myself to the task of studying," he wrote. "I spent long hours over my books and everything else was forgotten in my desire to get my education." On the wall of Naismith's room was a small sign expressing the motto he followed throughout his college years: "Do not let anybody work harder today than I do."

All of Naismith's freshman classes were required. Most students enjoyed the option of taking French, German, or Hebrew, but those who did not have at least one year of French or German in high school—Naismith among them—were required to take Hebrew. Naismith's study of Greek and Latin adequately prepared him for the class, but he still had some rough moments.

"This class came at 1 o'clock, and just after a good dinner, we were inclined to go to sleep," he reminisced. "Our instructor was a Breton from Normandy, a genial man of about 60. One day he gave me a sentence to put on the board. When it was translated it consisted of two words and I put them on the board and looked at him for his approval. He said, 'Very good, Mr. Naismith. Two words, two mistakes. I assume if you had some more words you would have some more mistakes.' I immediately brushed them off and wrote them correctly. He remarked, 'I knew you knew it, but you were asleep.'"

Naismith was in his room one evening, studying, when there was a knock on the door. He was surprised when two students he barely knew came in. After exchanging a greeting, one of them, Jim McFarland, spoke up. He was a junior and a fine athlete at McGill. The other student was Donald Dewar, also a junior but not an athlete.

"Naismith, we have been watching you for some time, and we see that you never take part in any of the activities," McFarland said. "You spend too much time with your books."

While McFarland was in good physical shape, Naismith could not say that about Dewar, who resembled an invalid. "Believe me, Naismith," Dewar said. "What McFarland says is true. I wouldn't listen to the fellows either, and you see the results."

The three students talked a while longer, and as McFarland and Dewar prepared to leave, Naismith thanked them for their advice. His first thought after they left, however, was negative: "I was sure that I was strong enough to study as hard as I wanted to and that I did not have time for sports."

Later that night, however, lying in bed before falling asleep, Naismith thought more about the advice. "The more I thought, the more clearly to my mind came the realization that they were doing it purely for my own benefit. I determined that the next day I would go over to the gymnasium and see what they were doing."

Naismith made his first visit to the McGill gymnasium the next afternoon, and that was where he met Frederick Barnjum, a legendary figure in physical education in Canada and the director of the McGill program. His presence made McGill one of the first universities in North America to recognize physical education as part of its regular curriculum. The activities were a perfect fit for Naismith, who soon became a regular participant.

"I had never been in a gymnasium in my life, but had been accustomed to climbing around the rafters of barns and buildings, and chinning myself to beat the other boys, and climbing ladders as a stunt, so any feats of strength were easy for me," Naismith recalled. "The work that required agility was more difficult. The pieces of apparatus that attracted me the most were the bridge ladder and the parallel bars."

After completing his freshman year, Naismith remembered his pledge to his uncle and returned to work on the farm, often working from daybreak, about 4 A.M., to sundown, which often came as late as 10 P.M. in the northern midsummer. Despite the long days and hard work, Naismith felt it was a worthy trade-off for his uncle's assuming the financial burden of his college education.

When he returned to McGill in the fall of 1884, Naismith had little idea that he was about to experience another life-altering event. Organized athletics were still fairly rare at the collegiate level, but the best team at McGill was the team that competed in English rugby, a variation of what was to grow into American football.

Returning to campus one evening after having gone downtown with a friend, Naismith stopped to watch the team practicing. During the scrimmage, the center broke his nose, and there was no substitute available. One of the team captains, Sack Elder, asked for volunteers among the spectators. No one stepped forward for a couple of minutes, until Naismith took off his coat and walked onto the field, where, he recalled later, "I did my best to fill the position."

At the end of practice, the captain asked Naismith if he would be able to take the place of the injured player for the game that Saturday against Queens University. Naismith agreed, on the condition that he could borrow that player's uniform. Each player was expected to provide his own uniform, and Naismith knew he could not get one before the game. The captain agreed, and Naismith was now a member of the rugby team, a position he would occupy for the next six years, during which he never missed a game.

By all accounts, Naismith was an immediate success on the rugby field. After the game against Queens, McGill played Toronto University. Naismith was singled out in the media for the quality of his play. The *McGill University Gazette* said that "a new scrimmage man, Naismith, very ably replaced Matthewson, whose nose had been put off the straight at a previous practice."

To play on the team required great dedication, as practice each day was at 6 A.M., and in late fall in Canada, the weather conditions were often brutal. The team could not practice later in the day because many of the students were in classes until dark. The sport also required some mental adjustments for Naismith, because he had been taught—and it was a popular opinion at the time—that athletics were "a tool of the devil."

Since he was planning to enter the School of Theology and become a minister, many fellow students could not understand how Naismith justified his participation on the rugby team. Naismith was amused by their opinions, including one time when he learned that a group of his friends had gathered to pray for his soul. Another person who would share their opinion, he knew, was his own sister, Annie.

Naismith's moral beliefs about drinking alcohol were also challenged by his participation on the rugby team. At the team banquet after his sophomore season, set out before each seat were a glass of white wine, one of red wine, one of whiskey, and one of brandy. "As I glanced around the table I could not find a single one who was not beginning on the course," Naismith later wrote. "My mind went back to the little book in the church and the phrase stuck to me 'as long as my name is on that book.' Had I been able I would have rushed out and had it removed, but that was impossible, and I spent two hours in hell, thinking that everyone at the table was thinking that I was a sissy. But the banquet ended and the glasses were untouched. Since that day I have had no trouble in refusing to drink."

There were times when some players on the team thought it would be funny to spike the ginger ale of the players who did not drink. "On one trip I recall sitting opposite a theolog who alternated between singing a ribald song and requesting that we would not tell he was drunk," Naismith said. "It was this side of football that put it into disfavor with the authorities of the Seminary and brought down on our heads the vote of censure. But the lure of the rough and tumble in the game and the desire to fight for the institution overcame the threats of the faculty and students and we kept on playing."

Whether Naismith and his sister talked about his athletic involvement when Naismith came back to the farm for the Christmas holiday in 1884 is not known. What is known is that Naismith was about to experience another personal tragedy. His brother Robbie, then 18, became ill, and nobody could determine what was wrong. Robbie went to bed on New Year's Eve complaining of a stomach ache, and the pain did not subside during the night.

When the rest of the family was out of the room, Robbie turned to his brother with a terrible request, which was to haunt Naismith for the rest of his life. "You wouldn't see a rabbit suffer like this and not kill it," Robbie Naismith said. "Why don't you kill me?"

Naismith, of course, had no intention of fulfilling that request. He wanted to help his brother, but he had no idea what to do. His older sister, Annie, had been the one to nurse the family through minor illnesses since their mother died, and she thought the proper treatment for a stomach ache was a dose of salts. Less than an hour later, Robbie Naismith was dead, having suffered a ruptured appendix.

The death of his brother devastated Naismith. Though nobody could replace Robbie, friendship with Tait McKenzie provided Naismith with as close a substitute as possible. McKenzie enrolled at McGill in the fall of 1885 and became Naismith's roommate. He quickly followed Naismith into the gymnasium and became a regular in the exercise classes.

"Jim and I used to linger after the class and try stunts," McKenzie wrote in later years. "In that way we learned the simpler forms of tumbling, the handspring and the back and front somersault, and in the course of time we worked up a brother act enriched from time to time by surreptitious visits to a vaudeville theater where there was usually a good acrobatic turn on the program. He was the under man, and I, being lighter, was top man. Many times he saved my neck by his steadiness."

The act grew, and when word spread to their hometown of Almonte, Naismith and McKenzie were asked to perform during the Christmas holidays as part of the program at the high school concert in the town hall. "Our act ended in a Catherine Wheel in which each held his partner's ankles, and by a series of dives rolled across the stage like a revolving wheel," McKenzie said. "We were accustomed to make six revolutions, but unfortunately, the stage was small and we found ourselves across before we realized it and too late to stop. So we burst through the dressing room door in the wings and collapsed in the midst of the chorus of girls who were changing their dresses."

McKenzie also recalled that Naismith was involved in other activities at McGill besides his studies, gymnastics, and rugby. "He was generally the leader of the raids and forages that fell upon the unsuspecting inhabitants of the 'west wing' in the college dormitory when study hours became too oppressive," McKenzie said. "On more than one occasion he had to appear before the 'powers' for explanation." Because of his academic and athletic success, however, the "powers" usually let Naismith go with nothing more than a warning and a slap on the wrist after he apologized for his actions.

Both Naismith and McKenzie joined the Fifth Royal Scots, which later became the Thirteenth Royal Canadian Highlanders. They went to marches wearing red coats and kilts. "On one occasion he brought me home ignominiously in a cab after I had disgraced myself by fainting in the drill hall after a long march," McKenzie said. "I had started with a sprained ankle which had swollen under the strain of the march in a tightly laced boot."

It was at the football field, however, that McKenzie and others were most lavish in their praise for Naismith's accomplishments. "He outplayed men who outweighed him by many pounds," McKenzie recalled. "Often I have seen him so exhausted after a game that he could hardly hold up his head, but in the game he was quick, resourceful, and could usually outwit his opponents."

On November 6, 1886, Naismith and the McGill team faced Queens College despite brutal weather conditions. The game was played in a blizzard, and after a scoreless first half, McGill took advantage of a favorable wind in the second half to pull out a 10–0 victory. Similarly, that year's game against the University of Toronto was played with several inches of snow on the ground, and more snow fell during the game.

One night, Naismith recalled, after a particularly tough game, his head fell over to one side at dinner. "When I attempted to straighten it up with my hand, it fell over to the other side. It was impossible for me to hold my head up for a couple of days. There were neither trainers or rubbers to take care of our injuries and we got well the best way we could."

During his junior and senior years, Naismith maintained his dual commitment to athletics and to his goal of becoming a minister. He spent the three summer months of 1886 working in the Canadian province of Manitoba as a missionary. As a gift, his new friends presented him with an engraved pocket watch that he took back to McGill in the fall. He continued to excel in athletics as well, winning the school's award as the best all-around gymnastics competitor as a junior and again as a senior.

Naismith was involved in other sports as well, including soccer, lacrosse, and boxing. In addition to intramural soccer games, McGill played games against city teams in which Naismith often participated. As a senior, he joined the Montreal Shamrocks, a professional lacrosse team. He learned to box by rising early in the morning when a group of students enlisted the services of a man named Jimmy Latter. "We got up at 6 A.M. and walked down [to Latter's barn] when the thermometer was 20 degrees below zero to learn the gentle art," Naismith wrote. "I have never regretted those hours spent and the journeys made in the cold and snow. I wish that every student could have a good course in boxing."

On April 30, 1887, Naismith received his bachelor's degree. He then enrolled in Presbyterian College at McGill, another step closer to the ministry, but he chose to continue his athletic involvement. In fact, his involvement increased when McGill's legendary physical education director, Frederick Barnjum, died, and the university asked Naismith to take over his classes. Naismith agreed to do so as a way to finance his own education in the Seminary.

Some of his fellow students, as well as teachers in the Seminary, continued to be upset that Naismith was so heavily involved in athletics, particularly that he played for the football team. In one rough game against Ottawa, Naismith suffered several bruises. The next morning, as a student minister, he climbed into a Presbyterian pulpit sporting two black eyes. His eyes were still black the next day when he showed up for his class in Old Testament Literature and Exegesis.

Despite the protests of his classmates and teachers, Naismith could not bring himself to the conclusion that being a Christian, and studying to be a minister, meant that he should not play and enjoy sports and athletics. His belief was reinforced by the appearance at McGill of a man from Yale University, Amos Alonzo Stagg, who delivered a lecture in which he said, in part, that it took many of the same qualities to become a good athlete as it did to become a good Christian, including enthusiasm, perseverance, and hard work.

At about the same time, Naismith was involved in a few incidents on the football field that convinced him even more that he should find a way to combine his work in athletics and the ministry. During a game between McGill and the Montreal Athletic Club, the McGill quarterback suffered a broken nose. McGill did not have a substitute to take his place. When the captain of the Montreal team heard this, he immediately said his team would remove its quarterback to make the two sides equal. The McGill quarterback then decided, however, that he would be able to play and, with that news, the Montreal captain gathered his team members around him and told them to "be careful" in playing against the injured quarterback. "I have always considered this one of the finest examples of sportsmanship that I have seen," Naismith said.

When one of his fellow football players, nicknamed "Drunken" Donegan, taunted Naismith for reading the Bible instead of going out with other members of the team and called him a sissy, Naismith floored him with one punch.

During Naismith's senior year at the Seminary, when McGill was involved in a close football game, the team's left guard, positioned next to Naismith, lost his temper and began to swear. "Suddenly he turned to me and said, 'I beg your pardon, Jim, I forgot you were there,'" Naismith said. "This surprised me more than a little. It was the first time that any man had ever apologized for swearing in my presence and it came as a queer sensation, as I had never said a word about profanity or any other subject that might have been construed as objecting to its use.

"Later, thinking the matter over, the only reason that I could give for the guard's action was that I played the game with all my might and yet held myself under control. . . . I was never considered a goody-goody boy but took my knocks in life or in athletics with a grin."

These episodes brought Naismith to the realization that he might perhaps provide more service to young men through athletics than through the traditional activities of the ministry. "My attention was directed to the fact that there were other ways of influencing young people than preaching," Naismith wrote in a letter in 1928. "In games it was easily seen that the man who took his part in a manly way and yet kept his thoughts and conduct clean had the respect and the confidence of the most careless. It was a short step to the conclusion that hard clean athletics could be used to set a high standard of living for the young."

He sought out the secretary of the Montreal YMCA, Mr. D. A. Budge, and told him about the incidents and his conclusions and asked Budge for advice. The Montreal YMCA (Young Men's Christian Association) had opened in 1851—the first North American branch of the organization founded in London in 1844. Budge and Naismith had become friends over the years during Naismith's frequent visits to the Y. Now Budge told Naismith about a school in Springfield, Massachusetts, that was developing and educating men to work in the field. Interested, Naismith vowed to learn more about the school.

The School for Christian Workers had been founded in 1885, and two years later a department of physical training had been added. In 1890 the school changed its name to the YMCA Training School, and a year afterward it became the International YMCA Training School. (In later years the institution's name changed twice more: to the International YMCA College in 1912, and then to Springfield College in 1954.) In Naismith's time, the school offered a two-year program of instruction that combined spiritual with physical development, preparing graduates to work and teach at the YMCA, in schools, churches, youth organizations, and other locations. YMCA branches were spreading quickly; the first in the United States had opened in Boston in 1851 only a few months after the one opened in Montreal.

Naismith also went to visit with one of his favorite professors to ask for his advice, and that teacher told him, "Naismith, I can't tell you what you should do. While this new field appears good, I would finish the course in theology; then if you do not like this new work, you can return to your original field."

Naismith got more advice from his longtime friend, Tait McKenzie, as he wrestled with the decision about whether to abandon his goal of becoming a minister. "There were many debates before he decided to give up the pulpit for physical education," McKenzie said. "It took courage at that time to leave the time honored and well beaten path for unknown and comparatively unexplored regions, but the decision once taken he never faltered, and I think, never regretted it."

Ultimately, Naismith decided that if his goal in life was to help educate and train young people, he could be of more value and potentially reach more people by working in athletics than he could by becoming the minister of a single church.

Naismith did follow his professor's advice by completing his theology work. He received his degree on April 18, 1890, making him eligible to accept a call to a pastorate. Instead, he spent the summer visiting several YMCAs in Canada and the United States, and stopping, unannounced, at the school in Springfield.

Most of his friends, and even his sister Annie and Uncle Peter, criticized him for passing up the ministry. "You put your hand to the plough," Annie told him, "and then turned back." He knew in his heart, however, that it was the right decision. "I became convinced that a great work could be done along this line and determined to attend the training school at Springfield."

When he arrived at Springfield, Naismith asked to meet with the dean of the physical education department, Dr. Luther Gulick,

Jr., but was told he was in class. Naismith sat down to wait for him. "I had been brought up in a British university, where all the professors with whom I was acquainted were elderly men, sedate and dignified," Naismith later described the scene. "After I had waited a few minutes, a man about my own age entered the office. He was tall and angular, his eyes were a bright piercing blue, and his hair and whiskers were a peculiar shade of carroty red. The man crossed the room with a rapid, jerky stride, fingered the mail on his desk, and then crossed to where I sat. With a winning smile on his face and a freckled hand extended, he welcomed me to the school. It is little wonder that I immediately felt a warm regard for Dr. Gulick, and I knew that with this man as dean of the school, I was going to enjoy my work."

Naismith went back to Almonte for the rest of the summer. He met two other Canadians, T. D. Patton of Ottawa and Dave Corbett of Montreal, who also had enrolled in the school in Springfield. The three headed south in September, ready for the new challenges in a new country.

"I felt that there was a new field in which good could be done for mankind as well as in preaching and that some people would be able to do better work in one field than the other," Naismith said. "Athletics and gymnastics at that time were looked on as a device of the devil to lead young men astray. I felt, however, that if the devil was making use of them to lead young men, it must have some natural attraction, and that it might be used to lead to a good end as well as to a bad one."

CHAPTER 3

. . .

The Springfield Challenge— and a New Game

One of the first things Naismith did after arriving in Springfield in the fall of 1890 was to see Dr. Gulick. Walking into the dean's office, he found Gulick sitting at his desk, talking to another young man. Gulick immediately stood up and introduced Naismith to another student coming into the school that fall—Amos Alonzo Stagg.

Stagg had been an All-America football player at Yale, and a theological student, and it was natural that he and Naismith would become great friends because they shared many of the same ideas and philosophies about life and athletics. Like Naismith, Stagg and Gulick were both in their twenties, and the three were united in their beliefs that they had been called not only to train young men in athletics, but to build men of strong value and character.

It was Gulick, the son of a missionary in Hawaii, who invented the Y's inverted triangle symbol, representing the mind, body, and spirit. At his own expense, he founded a newspaper for the Y called the *Triangle* in 1891. Naismith was to recall years later that Gulick "was one of the few men whose teachings have remained with me and have been a help not only in my profession but in my life as well."

Stagg, like Naismith, had been educated to become a minister but had turned down the opportunity to accept a pastorate in favor of working with young men in the field of athletics. A star pitcher at Yale, Stagg also turned down an offer to sign professionally in that sport with the New York Giants.

Possibly because of Stagg's presence, Gulick decided to start a football team at the YMCA Training School and appointed Stagg as the coach. Thirteen students, including Naismith, from the school's enrollment of 57 men were selected to play on the team.

"Just before the opening game, I had my first view of the man who, through the years, has become the dean of American football," Naismith wrote. "It was in the dressing room, just before we were to go out on the field. Stagg had given us our instructions, then he turned to us and said, 'Let us ask God's blessing on our game.'

"He did not pray for victory, but he prayed that each man should do his best and show the true Christian spirit."

It was no surprise that the team became known as "Stagg's Stubby Christians" as they competed against Harvard, Yale, Amherst, and other eastern colleges and universities in 1890 and 1891. Naismith played center on the team, as he had done at McGill.

"I recognized Stagg's ability as a coach and noticed that he would pick one man for a position and keep him there," Naismith said. "He seemed to have the uncanny ability to place the right man in the right position. I asked him one day how it happened that he played me at center. Stagg looked at me and in a serious voice replied, 'Jim, I play you at center because you can do the meanest things in the most gentlemanly manner.'"

The outmanned squad's game against Yale caught the attention of New York sportswriters. In a story on October 18, 1891, the *New York Times* reported, "It has been said that Yale methods and training in football will make good players out of ordinary material. A test of this, perhaps, is given in the practice games with the second class elevens from the smaller colleges. With an eleven that has not had the benefit of Yale training, the Yale eleven can do about what it pleases; while with an eleven like that from Springfield, trained by Stagg, the wearers of the blue had a struggle which strained their muscles, sprained their limbs, and brought out all that was in them. That game with Stagg's eleven lessened somewhat the feeling of confidence in Yale's prowess previously entertained, and showed the necessity of hard work under careful coaching if the football superiority is to be wrested from Harvard and Princeton."

Naismith and Stagg developed a close friendship that was to last the rest of their lives. Both completed the two-year course at Springfield in one year, and both were asked to remain the following year as members of the faculty.

It was during the 1891 season that Naismith is credited by many with inventing the forerunner of the modern football helmet, a move that came out of necessity. Because he played center, Naismith was always getting hit in the head by opponents trying to get past him to the quarterback. The constant blows were giving Naismith a cauliflower ear. (Years later, his passport listed such an ear as one of his "identifying features.") Worse, during a game against the Connecticut Literary Institute, he suffered an injury that convinced him preventive measures were needed. The Springfield team won, 32–0, but as the Springfield newspaper reported, "Soon after the game began, Captain Naismith of the training school, while running with the ball, fell forward and was kicked accidentally by a man running near him. He was stunned and lost his memory, not recognizing his friends on the field. He was carefully tended Saturday night and yesterday morning was nearly recovered."

Naismith found some pieces of flannel, and his girlfriend (and future wife), Maude Sherman, stitched a makeshift helmet together, making sure it was big enough to cover his ears. When he first wore the contraption onto the practice field, Stagg said to him, "What are you going to do, butt like a goat?" The device, however primitive it looked, did help protect Naismith's ears and head from further injury. Later he used the leather of an old rugby football to make a stronger helmet.

Football was one of the few organized sports available to young men at the time. Baseball and track took place in the spring and summer. Once it got too cold to be outdoors in the winter, there was little for men to do except work in the gymnasium, and the students at Springfield, like those in other schools, quickly became bored with gymnastics, calisthenics, and other similar activities. All of the Springfield teachers were aware of the growing unease of the students, but none of them had any ideas about what to do to solve the problem.

"We needed some sort of game that would be interesting and could be played indoors," Naismith recalled. "We had three games—three-deep, line ball and Dr. Gulick's game called cricket. We had a seminar in which we discussed those things quite frequently. It was a seminar in psychology, and one day in discussing inventions Dr. Gulick made this statement: 'There is nothing new under the sun, but all new things are simply a re-combination of the factors of existing things.' After thinking it over, I said to Dr. Gulick, 'If that is true, we can go to work to invent a new game.' Nothing much more was said about it, but Dr. Stagg said he assigned that as our home work for the next meeting, but no one brought in any record at all."

Dr. Gulick's instructions about the requirements for the new game were fairly simple. "We need a new game to exercise our students," Gulick said, "a competitive game, like football or lacrosse, but it must be a game that can be played indoors. It must be a game requiring skill and sportsmanship, providing exercise for the whole body and yet it must be one which can be played without extreme roughness or damage to players and equipment."

Naismith admired Dr. Gulick a great deal, and he thought the two of them made a good team. He talked often about the inspiration he received from Gulick. "In one discussion, he saw a

vision of some project, and I suggested that the thing to do was to begin in a remote way to reach the point. Gulick said, 'Naismith, you are nothing but an obstructionist.' I understood his attitude and answered, 'I am not an obstructionist, but a pathfinder.' At this remark, we both laughed."

Trying to find some physical activity to keep the Springfield students entertained and occupied in the winter months, however, was no laughing matter. Gulick sent Naismith on a trip to Martha's Vineyard, Massachusetts, to study the principles of the Swedish system of exercise, being taught there by Baron Nils Posse.

Naismith and Baron Posse discussed the needs of the YMCA students. Naismith also observed the Baron's classes and made many notes, which he shared with Dr. Gulick on his return to Springfield. While the two agreed that there were many positive aspects to the Swedish training—many parts of which they later began using in their own classes—it did not solve the problem of occupying the men during the winter months.

At the time, the students at the Training School were divided into two groups, those who were training to become physical directors and those who were training to be secretaries, or administrators, of the Y. "At the close of the outdoor sports, all the students went to the gymnasium for their exercise," Naismith wrote. "The physical directors and the secretaries did their work in separate classes. The first were interested in getting as much as possible out of their regular class work, because it trained them for their profession. The secretaries, however, had a different attitude toward physical activities—they had all the physical development they needed and were not interested. They were, nevertheless, required to spend an hour each day in what was to most of them distasteful work."

One class of secretarial students presented a particular problem. That class of 18 students went through two instructors, A. T. Halstead and Robert Clark. Halstead was an expert in marching and mass calisthenics, but as he tried to emphasize those top-

ics, he could generate little interest among the students. When he asked to be relieved of the class, Gulick assigned the class to Clark, whom Naismith considered the best gymnast and athlete among the faculty members. Clark had been a Phi Beta Kappa at Williams College and had earned a medical degree. His first actions with the class were to drop all marching and calisthenics, and he had the students begin working on the various pieces of gymnastics apparatus. They played games such as potato races and other childhood amusements. "Here again, the men were given exercise in which they had no interest," Naismith said. "Try as hard as he could, Clark failed to arouse any enthusiasm for the work that had been intensely interesting to the classes he had taught before."

Clark reported back to the faculty meeting that he believed he too was failing with the class and asked to be relieved of the assignment. Naismith spoke up, saying, "The trouble is not with the men, but with the system we are using. The kind of work for this particular class should be of a recreational nature, something that would appeal to their play interests."

The rest of the faculty was quiet, each person trying desperately to think of a solution. Naismith knew what was needed—a game that could be played indoors and generate the enthusiasm that football and baseball created outdoors. But no such game existed. All of the indoor games at this time were virtually child-appropriate games, and he understood why college-age and adult men found them boring and repetitive.

It was late November, and Naismith was busy teaching his classes, which at this point included psychology and Bible study as well as the sports of boxing, wrestling, swimming, and canoeing. The last thing he expected after he spoke up was for Gulick to turn to him and say, "Naismith, I want you to take that class and see what you can do with it."

Naismith was stunned. He did not want to give up teaching the sports he enjoyed, particularly swimming and canoeing, to teach a group that was becoming known as the "incorrigible"

class. He tried to get out of the assignment, but Gulick was adamant. He gave Naismith two weeks to see what he could do with the class, and as Naismith said, "My fate was sealed."

After the meeting, Naismith was walking down the hall when Gulick came up beside him. Gulick knew Naismith was upset, and he wanted to offer him some encouragement and reassurance. He thought he was doing so when he said, "Now would be a good time for you to work on that new game you said could be invented."

Naismith, however, took Gulick's statement as an imposition. Not only was he given the toughest teaching assignment in the school, he was also being handed the responsibility of inventing a new game—a task that had so far stumped all of the instructors.

"If I ever tried to back out of anything, I did then," Naismith said. "I did not want to do it. . . . I have never found out whether it was intentional on the part of Dr. Gulick to unite the two difficulties, or merely incidental, to get rid of two vexing problems, that he gave both of them to the same person; but it is certain that they worked together for ultimate good."

Naismith no doubt had a few unpleasant thoughts toward Dr. Gulick, who had so impressed him from the moment of their first meeting. He realized later that Gulick had issued the challenge because he expected Naismith to complete the task—as Naismith had first learned to do on his uncle's farm as a young boy.

Resigned to his task, Naismith tried to make the best of it. He knew the class was filled with older students, and if he had been put in their place, he knew he might very well have acted in the same manner. He was not mad or angry at them. He quickly learned that the two leaders of the class were T. D. Patton, a fellow Canadian, and Frank Mahan, a burly Irishman from North Carolina who had played tackle on the school's football team. Naismith could tell immediately that whatever activity they approved would be accepted by the rest of the class.

For the first part of his two-week assignment, Naismith tried to interest the class in every existing game he could think of.

Though he stressed recreation rather than instruction, all the games failed to hold the interest of the class.

"This class was different from any other in the institution," Naismith wrote. "They were mature men, physically well developed by their previous life. They were not interested in learning to do stunts for exhibition purposes . . . nor were they interested in learning to conduct classes. Yet they were required to take the same kind of work as the physical men.

"I did not blame the men for being rebellious under the circumstances. Indeed I have no doubt but had I been a member of their class I would have joined the rebels and have done my best to get rid of the obnoxious requirement."

Naismith next tried to modify outdoor games to see if they could be played indoors. He first turned to football, but even with a modified form of tackling it proved to be too rough. "To ask these men to handle their opponents gently was to make their favorite sport a laughing stock and they would have none of it," Naismith said.

He then tried soccer, which was called Association football at the time. He thought that kicking with a soft-soled shoe would lessen the number of injuries, but this also proved to be wishful thinking. Trying that sport resulted in a "practical lesson in first aid," he said. "Some of the former soccer players had learned to drive the ball with the inside of the foot, and if they missed their shots at the goal, they were likely to smash the windows, which were at that time unscreened. There were times when the game waxed so furious that it was necessary to call time out in order that we could remove the clubs and the dumbbells that were knocked from the racks on the wall."

Soccer, like football, was quickly dropped from the list of potential indoor games. "I had pinned my hopes on these two games, and when they failed me, there seemed little chance of success," Naismith said. "Each attempt was becoming more difficult."

Naismith thought back to other games he had played, and the next one he tried to modify for indoor play was lacrosse. He thought the sport might work with a modified, shorter crosse, similar to a racquet, but since he didn't have the time or money necessary to make such an invention, he decided to play the game with regular crosses.

"In the group were seven Canadians, and when these men put into practice some of the tricks they had been taught in the outdoor game, football and soccer appeared tame in comparison," Naismith wrote. "No bones were broken in the game, but faces were scarred and hands were hacked. Those who had never played the game were unfortunate, for it was these men to whom the flying crosses did the most damage. The beginners were injured and the experts were disgusted: another game went into the discard."

Naismith was down to the last couple of days before he had to report back to the faculty. "How I hated the thought of going back to the group and admitting that, after all my theories, I, too, had failed to hold the interest of the class," he later disclosed. "It was worse than losing a game. All the stubbornness of my Scotch ancestry was aroused, all my pride of achievement urged me on; I would not go back and admit that I had failed. . . . It was time to put up or shut up. I was determined to put up and not shut up."

Naismith thought about other attempts he had heard and read about to invent a new indoor game. Dr. Sergent at Harvard had invented a game called battle ball, in which the men of one team set up clubs and the other team threw balls to try to knock them down. Dr. Gulick himself had invented a game with a partition stretched across the floor, the goal of the game being to throw a medicine ball over the partition and have it touch the floor on the other side before the opponents caught it. Dr. Gulick also had invented a modified game of cricket. None of those games had been successful either.

On the next-to-last day of his two-week assignment, Naismith met the class with no idea of what they were going to do for the 60-minute period. He gave the students no instructions, leaving them on their own. When the period ended, Naismith watched solemnly as they filed out of the gym and into the locker room. With them, he thought, went "the end of all my ambitions and hopes."

"With weary footsteps I mounted the flight of narrow stairs that led to my office directly over the locker room," he wrote. "I slumped down in my chair, my head in my hands and my elbows on the desk. I was a thoroughly disheartened and discouraged young instructor. Below me, I could hear the boys in the locker room having a good time; they were giving expression to the very spirit that I had tried so hard to evoke."

As he listened to the locker-room chatter through the narrow floor, Naismith tried to retrace his attempts of the previous two weeks to develop a game that would interest the class. One by one he reviewed the games he had tried, and reasoned out why they had failed. He realized that his attempts to modify existing games had failed because the students, and other athletes, enjoyed those games as they were and did not want to mess with tradition.

Continuing to sit at his desk, even after the students had left the locker room and moved on to their next class, Naismith next thought about games "from the philosophical side." Pondering games as a whole, rather than individually, he started to draw some conclusions.

All team games that he could think of involved a ball. So, whatever new game was to be invented should have a ball of some kind. What were the differences in the types of balls? One basic difference was size. The games that used a small ball needed extra equipment, such as baseball, cricket, hockey, lacrosse, tennis, and squash. The more equipment that was involved, the harder the game would be to learn and to play. Since Dr. Gulick had instructed him that a new game should be easy to learn and accessible to many people, a small ball seemed out of the question. Another problem with a small ball, he realized, was that it could easily be hidden in a player's clothes, and nobody would know who had the ball.

Thinking about large balls, two came to Naismith's mind: a spheroid like the ones used in rugby and football and the round ball used in soccer. Either one of those likely would work in a new game.

The second question Naismith considered was the innate interest of the sport. The most popular game of that era, not only among his students but among the population in general, was American rugby. Why couldn't this sport be played indoors? The answer was easy—the sport was too rough. Tackling somebody running with the ball would result in far too many injuries if the sport were played in a gymnasium. Why was tackling necessary? To stop the man running with the ball.

"With these facts in mind, I sat erect at my desk and said aloud, 'If he can't run with the ball, we don't have to tackle,'" Naismith later wrote. "'If we don't have to tackle, the roughness will be eliminated.' I can still recall how I snapped my fingers and shouted, 'I've got it.'"

Years later, Naismith would remember that moment and wonder why he was so elated. All he had, basically, was one principle of a new game, that the men could not run with the ball. That was hardly the framework for a new sport. He knew, however, that finally he was on to something.

If a player could not run with the ball, what could he do with it? There were only two choices that Naismith could think of: he had to throw it or bat it with his hand. If he threw it to another man who was running, it would be hard for that man to stop immediately. Naismith decided that the second man would either have to make an honest attempt to stop or immediately throw the ball to another player.

"In my mind I was still sticking to the traditions of the older games, especially football," Naismith admitted. "In that game, the ball could be thrown in any direction except forward. In this new game, however, the player with the ball could not advance, and I saw no reason why he should not be allowed to throw or bat it in any direction."

When Naismith imagined trying to defend a player who was passing the ball, he visualized a man striking the ball with his first, and intentionally or not, having his fist collide with an opponent's face. Defenders would not be allowed to strike the ball with their fists, he quickly decided.

What Naismith had invented, so far, was a form of "keep away." The next step was to create some other objective for the players. Thinking again of other sports, Naismith realized they all contained some type of goal or finish line. What he thought would work best with his new game was a goal similar to the one used in lacrosse, a net six feet high and eight feet wide—one on each end of the floor.

A team would score a goal when a player threw the ball into the net. The harder the ball was thrown, the better chance he would have of scoring. However, Naismith reasoned, that arrangement might once again raise the likelihood of injuries. But what other possibility for a goal existed?

Naismith's mind wandered back to his days behind the blacksmith shop in Bennie's Corners. What was his favorite game? Duck on the Rock. Why was it fun? The players had to throw a stone and try to knock another stone off a high rock. The players who successfully knocked the stone away were not the ones who could throw the hardest, but the ones who were the most accurate. That was the kind of principle that Naismith was striving to find.

"I thought that if the goal were horizontal instead of vertical, the players would be compelled to throw the ball in an arc," Naismith wrote. "Force, which made for roughness, would be of no value."

Naismith tried to picture the goals in his mind. What he envisioned was a pair of boxes, one on each end of the gym floor. Each time the ball was thrown into a box, a goal would be scored. Picturing his class of incorrigibles, though, he realized that if nine men were guarding the goal, there would be little chance that an opposing player would be able to score. The goals would have to be elevated above the defenders' heads, so they could not all stand in front of the goal and block it.

By this time, Naismith knew he was getting closer to developing the basic framework of a new game. The emerging game seemed entertaining and competitive and had an objective. The next question was how to start the game.

He thought of water polo, in which the teams lined up on each end of the pool and a ball was thrown into the middle. This wouldn't work in the gym, again because of the possibility of injury. He next thought of English rugby: when a ball went out of bounds, the referee rolled it back in play between two lines of players. The players did not have time to run at each other, but injuries might still occur. "I remembered one incident that happened to me," Naismith recounted. "In a game with Queens College, the ball was thrown between the two lines of players. I took one step and went high in the air. I got the ball all right, but as I came down, I landed on a shoulder that was shoved into my midriff. I decided that this method would not do."

Throwing a ball up between the two teams, however, seemed to him to be the fairest way to start the game. If one player were selected from each team for that jump, there seemed to Naismith to be little chance of injury.

The framework of the game was now in place, and Naismith believed it would meet all of Dr. Gulick's requirements. About the only thing he had not decided was which ball to use. For the first time in two weeks, he went to bed with a smile on his face and slept soundly through the night.

• • •

CHAPTER 4

The Game Is Born

A s Naismith arrived at his office the next morning, he picked up a football and soccer ball. He noticed how the football was shaped so it could be carried in the arms. Since running with the ball would not be allowed in his new game, Naismith chose to use the soccer ball.

Next, he had to find a couple of goals. As he walked down the hall of the gymnasium, he approached the superintendent of the building, Pop Stebbins, and asked if Pop had a couple of boxes about 18 inches square that he could use. "No," Stebbins said, hesitating for a moment, "but I'll tell you what. I have a couple of peach baskets about that size down in the store room if that will do you any good."

In his handwritten notes about the first game, Naismith said, "I asked him to bring them up to the gym floor. I nailed them to the gallery, one at each end, and the equipment was ready."

The lower railing of the gallery happened to be 10 feet high. Naismith said later if the railing had been 11 feet high, that's how high the goals would have been.

Returning to his office, Naismith sat at his desk, pulled out a piece of paper, and drafted the original rules for his new game in less than an hour. Specifying that the ball would be an ordinary Association football, he came up with 13 rules:

1. The ball may be thrown in any direction with one or both hands.
2. The ball may be batted in any direction with one or both hands (never with the fist).
3. A player cannot run with the ball. The player must throw it from the spot on which he catches it; allowance to be made for a man who catches the ball when running at a good speed.
4. The ball must be held in or between the hands; the arms or body must not be used for holding it.
5. No shouldering, holding, pushing, tripping, or striking in any way the person of an opponent shall be allowed; the first infringement of this rule by any person shall count as a foul; the second shall disqualify him until the next goal is made, or, if there was evident intent to injure the person, for the whole of the game, no substitute allowed.
6. A foul is striking at the ball with the fist, violation of rules 3, 4 and such as described in rule 5.
7. If either side makes three consecutive fouls, it shall count as a goal for the opponents (consecutive means without the opponents in the meantime making a foul).
8. A goal shall be made when the ball is thrown or batted from the grounds into the basket and stays there, providing those defending the goal do not touch or disturb the goal. If the ball rests on the edge and the opponent moves the basket, it shall count as a goal.
9. When the ball goes out of bounds, it shall be thrown into the field and played by the person first touching it. In case of a dispute, the umpire shall throw it straight into the field. The thrower-in is allowed five

seconds. If he holds it longer it shall go to the opponent. If any side persists in delaying the game, the umpire shall call a foul on them.

10. The umpire shall be the judge of the men and shall note the fouls and notify the referee when three consecutive fouls have been made. He shall have the power to disqualify men according to rule 5.

11. The referee shall be the judge of the ball and shall decide when the ball is in play, in bounds, to which side it belongs, and shall keep the time. He shall decide when a goal has been made, and keep account of the goals, with any other duties that are usually performed by a referee.

12. The time shall be two fifteen minute halves, with five minutes rest in between.

13. The side making the most goals in that time shall be declared the winners. In case of a draw, the game may, by agreement of the captains, be continued until another goal is made.

Naismith gave the rules to Miss Lyons, the stenographer, who typed them and gave them back to him. It was almost 11:30 A.M., the starting time for the class. He took the rules and, just inside the door, fastened them with thumb tacks on the bulletin board.

"I was sure in my mind that the game was good, but it needed a real test," Naismith wrote. "I felt that its success or failure depended largely on the way that the class received it."

Carrying a soccer ball, Naismith called the 18 students together to explain the new game they were going to play. The sport of basketball—although it did not yet have that name—was about to be born.

Naismith's nerves were raging. In his handwritten notes, he said, "I felt that this was a crucial moment in my life as it meant success or failure of my attempt to hold the interest of the class and devise a new game. I had neither the advantage of age nor the benefit for experience to help me put this across."

On that cold New England winter morning, December 21, 1891, Naismith was merely trying to please 18 students. He had no long-term plan in mind. His motives were simple, plain, and direct.

Mahan was the first of the students to gather around Naismith. He saw the ball in his hand, then glanced to one end of the gym and saw the peach basket nailed to the gallery railing. He looked toward the other end of the gym and saw another basket. He then looked back at Naismith.

"Perhaps I was nervous, because his exclamation sounded like a death knell as he said, 'Huh, another new game!'" Naismith wrote. "While this was rather discouraging, it did not alter my opinion of the game."

Naismith took roll and briefly explained the new game. He had the students review the rules, and he promised them that if the game was not a success, he would not burden them with any additional experiments. The class was wearing its regular gym clothes, no special uniforms. The lights in the gym were dim, and there were no markings or boundaries painted or taped to the floor. The only out-of-bounds areas for the 60-foot by 35-foot gym were the walls and the places where the dumbbells and gymnastics apparatus were stored.

Two captains were selected—Eugene Libby and T. D. Patton—and each picked the players for his team, nine on each side. Naismith positioned the players around the floor as in lacrosse. He tossed the ball in the air, two players jumped for it, and the new game was born.

"After a very few minutes of play there was no question in the mind of the experimenter [himself] but that the game would be a success," Naismith wrote. "The players seemed to heartily enjoy the rough and tumble of the game, especially the effort to keep from personal contact with the opponents."

It took the players some time to understand how best to play the game and avoid fouls. The most common problem was a player's starting to run with the ball after he had caught a pass, a natural instinct. That was considered a foul, and the rules sent offending players to the sidelines until the next goal was made. "Sometimes half of a team would be in the penalty area," Naismith noted.

"No one knew just what to do," he continued. "There was no team work at first, but each man tried to do his best. The forwards tried to make goals and the backs tried to keep the opponents from making goals. The floor was small and the team was large; any man on the floor was close enough to the basket to shoot, but we tried to have the guards pass the ball to the forwards."

Y secretary-to-be William Chase scored the first, and only, basket in the first game—on a toss from about 25 feet away. Naismith had anticipated the problem of getting the ball out of the basket, so he had asked Stebbins to be ready, with his stepladder, to climb up and retrieve the ball.

When time expired and the class period was over, Naismith breathed a large sigh of relief. The game had been so successful, in fact, that the students did not want to stop. They wanted to keep playing rather than move on to their next class.

"I could go to Dr. Gulick and tell him that I could 'put up.'" Naismith wrote. "I didn't have to 'shut up.' I had accomplished the two seemingly impossible tasks that he had assigned me, namely to interest the class in physical education and to invent a new game."

Word soon spread throughout the school that the men in the class were playing a new game. People started showing up in the gallery to watch. Within two weeks as many as 200 people filled the gallery during the class period. That group included a number of female teachers from the nearby Buckingham Grade School, who passed by the gym's open door during their lunch break, heard the commotion, and came inside to watch the game.

Naismith and his sister Annie, in a photo taken when Naismith was about three years old. They were raised by their uncle after their parents died when Naismith was a young boy.

It was while Naismith was a student at McGill University that he discovered the true joy and satisfaction that come from participating in athletics.

Naismith graduated from McGill University in 1887 and was proud of his accomplishments, believing that he had repaid the trust his uncle placed in him when he left the family farm in pursuit of an education.

Above: After Naismith moved to the YMCA Training School (later Springfield College) in 1890 to learn to become a YMCA administrator, he joined Amos Alonzo Stagg's "Flying Christians" football team.

Below: Students at the YMCA Training School who participated in the first basketball game ever played, posing for a picture in 1891. These students were members of Naismith's graduating class.

One of the reasons Naismith was so pleased with the invention of basketball was the game's popularity among women, who he thought could play the game as well as men.

One of the beauties of basketball, Naismith believed, was the minimal need for equipment: a basketball and a basket, along with a place to play. In the beginning, that was all they had.

Above: Because of the missionaries sent overseas by the YMCA, the international growth of basketball was exceptional. One of the first countries to pick up the game was Japan, where this gym was prepared for the competitors to come.

Below: The first recorded basketball game in Japan was played in 1915 in Kobe between a team from that city and a team from Kyoto. Spectators, as well as the players, had to learn the rules of the new game.

Naismith and his wife, Maude, shown in a 1927 photo, could not believe how much the game had changed in a very short time after its invention in 1891. Maude participated in one of the first women's games ever played.

After a few days of watching, some of the teachers approached Naismith and asked if they could play the game too. Naismith said he did not see any reason against it. The group organized the first women's basketball team, and they were assigned an hour later in the day when the gym was available.

"It was not long until the stenographers of the school got up another team," Naismith recalled in a 1932 speech in Springfield. "Some of us young unmarried men got our sweethearts interested in it and we got a ladies faculty team. The girls asked me to umpire. I agreed to but I didn't know as much about ladies as I do now. We got along nicely until I called a foul on one of the girls. She asked, 'Did you call a foul on me?' and then she told me where I came from, where I was going to, and what my character was. I tried to pacify her, but couldn't do it. The only thing to do was to toss up the ball and then she had to fall into her place.

"That girl was not different from other girls. They never had a chance to take part in any game where sportsmanship was required. It was something new for them. She had played some shuttle cock and a few other games similar to that; they had not even played tennis."

When Naismith saw that his new game was popular not only among the students in the incorrigibles class, but among women as well—and among people just coming to watch the game with no intention of playing the sport—his confidence in its long-term success grew. "It is little wonder that the crowd enjoyed the game," he reminisced in later years. "If we could see it today as it was played that first time we too would laugh. The players were all older men, most of them had moustaches and one or two had full beards. Their pants were long and their shirts had short sleeves. Often the player would receive the ball and pause with it over his head to make sure that the basket would be made. About the time that he was ready to shoot someone would reach up from behind the ball and take it out of his hands. This was a never ending source of amusement for no matter how often a player would lose the ball in this manner, he would look around with a surprised expression on his face as if to say, 'Who did that?'"

After the first game, the original rules that had been tacked to the bulletin board by the gym's door mysteriously disappeared. Naismith did not worry much about their absence, but a couple of weeks later Mahan approached Naismith before class and admitted that he had taken them. "I knew that this game was going to be a success and I took those rules as a souvenir," Mahan confessed, "but I think you ought to have them." Mahan retrieved the original rules from a trunk in his room and returned them to Naismith, who kept them in his possession the rest of his life—almost.

"One summer school I took them to a class to compare with the present rules and, putting them in my desk, I forgot all about them," Naismith revealed years later. "On looking for them some time later I could not find them and at last gave them up for lost. In looking over some of my files, twelve years later, I came across a long envelope with no name on it. On closer inspection, I discovered that it bore the heading dated some fifteen years past. This aroused my curiosity and on opening the packet, greatly to my delight, the rules came to view."

It was also Mahan, after the students returned from Christmas break, who asked Naismith if he had come up with a name for the new game. Naismith answered no, and Mahan suggested "Naismith ball." Naismith laughed, and said giving it a name like that would be a sure method of killing the game before it really got started.

Okay, Mahan responded. "We have a basket and we have a ball. How about basket ball?" Naismith thought this name sounded much better, and it quickly was adopted. The name continued to be spelled as two words until 1921, when sportswriters shortened it to one word.

Even before the game had a name, the students from the incorrigibles' class had begun to spread the word. Going to their various homes for the Christmas break, across the United States and into Canada, they took news of the game with them. Some went to local YMCAs and demonstrated how it was played.

Gulick's school newspaper, the *Triangle*, printed the first rules and story about basketball in the issue of January 1892, under the headline "A New Game." The newspaper was distributed to YMCAs throughout the United States and Canada.

As the popularity of the game grew within the Training School classes, the class of secretaries formed an organized team of nine players and challenged the class of physical directors to a game, ready to display their superiority. On the day of that game, "the gymnasium was filled to capacity," Naismith wrote. "The admirers of the young men of course cheered for the side on which their heroes were playing. This created a sense of rivalry and the general enthusiasm soon spread."

The secretaries won, and next looked for another team to beat. A team of faculty members was formed, and the secretary class beat them, too, by a score of 5 to 1. The lone faculty basket was scored by Amos Alonzo Stagg.

This game, played on March 11, 1892, is generally recognized as the first public game of basketball. A crowd of more than 200 people gathered in the gallery to watch. Naismith played in the game as a member of the faculty, one of only two times in his life that he actually played the game that he invented.

The *Springfield Republican* reported the next day that the most impressive member of the faculty team was Stagg, who, the newspaper noted, had a particularly tough time abandoning his football training. He was continually charged with fouls for shoving his opponents, and he received a black eye in retaliation for the bruises he inflicted. Naismith was also called for multiple fouls, no doubt because of his background in wrestling, lacrosse, and football.

Stagg admitted later that he really enjoyed the new game, but he was to become famous for coaching football at the University of Chicago, a position he accepted in July 1892. He coached at Chicago until 1932, and then at the College of the Pacific until

1946, when he was 84 years old. In 1943, at the age of 81, he was named the college coach of the year. Among the football innovations Stagg is credited with are the huddle by players on the field, the lateral pass, putting a man in motion, and putting players' names on the backs of their jerseys. He lived until he was 102 years old, dying in 1965.

After winning the game against the faculty, the team of students, captained by Mahan, soon began to travel and play exhibition games, often joining a group of other Training School students known as the "Flying Circus" who put on athletic performances.

The team played an exhibition game to open the athletic grounds of the New York YMCA, and basketball was mentioned for the first time in the *New York Times* on April 26, 1892, under the headline "A New Game of Ball, A Substitute for Football Without its Rough Features." The newspaper reported that the Springfield team had beaten the New York team 1–0, and also said two games would be played at the Y athletic grounds the following Saturday.

With the growth of the game came refinements in the playing conditions. The first change that had to be made—as all involved soon realized—was to find an easier way to get the ball out of the basket after a goal was made. During the first few games at the Training School, a spectator was asked to help out by reaching over the railing and taking the ball out of the basket whenever a goal was made. Because not many goals were scored, this person soon got bored and left. Next, a ladder was placed near each basket, and whenever the ball went in the basket, the game was stopped until someone climbed up to retrieve the ball.

History did not record who first came up with the idea of simply knocking out the bottom of each basket. It would not be until 1898 that iron rims, attached to nets, were used as goals to replace the baskets.

The second problem that needed attention occurred when the referee, standing on the side of the court, threw the ball in to start the game. From that distance, his aim often wasn't very good. It was decided to let the referee onto the court to toss the ball between two players to start the game. After the toss, he quickly retreated to the sidelines; it still didn't seem safe for the referee to remain on the court in the midst of 18 players.

More revisions came in the ensuing years. In 1893, the penalty for a foul was changed from sitting out until a goal was made; instead, the opponent was given one point. The free-throw system after fouls was added in 1894. The first "basketball" was made by the Overman Wheel Co., a bicycle manufacturing company in Chicopee Falls, Massachusetts. The new sphere was lighter and larger than the original soccer ball. In 1896, players on the Yale team were the first to use the dribble in competition. The field goal's value also was doubled, from one point to two. In 1897, the number of players on each side was reduced from nine to five. In 1901, the officials moved from the sidelines onto the court to regulate the game and call fouls and violations. The length of the games also changed over the years.

When the first set of rules was published in the January 1892 newspaper, so many requests for copies were received that the newspaper had to print a special booklet, which also listed the equipment necessary to play the game. There had been no mention of the ball, the goals, or the court requirements in the original rules.

Another change from Naismith's original rules, in the early years, was the addition of backboards behind the goals. With the fans sitting in the gallery behind the goals, it quickly became apparent to Naismith and others that a fan of one team had the ability, as a shot was coming toward the goal, to reach over the railing and knock the ball away. Rather than exclude fans from that area, or simply count the goal, the organizers placed a board behind the goal to block interference by the fans.

Nobody at the time realized that adding the backboard behind the goal would make it easier for the players to score goals, since they could miss the basket, hit the backboard, and still have the ball bounce into the goal. That was a nice fringe benefit of the change. The difference was also apparent in smaller gyms, without a gallery, where the goal had to be hung directly against a wall. If there was a railing on one end of the gym and only a wall on the other end, the team shooting at the goal hung to the wall had a distinct advantage.

In October 1892, Dr. Gulick wrote in the Training School notes that "It is doubtful whether a gymnastic game has ever spread so rapidly over the continent as has 'basket ball.' It is played from New York to San Francisco." Reports came in from New York, Rhode Island, and even Oregon about the success and popularity of the game. In April 1893, Naismith received a letter from Mrs. H. L. Carver in Greenville, Texas, asking for a copy of the rules and for more information about the game, saying she was "anxious to learn it and introduce it in Texas." It was only a few years before the game, spread by missionaries from the Y, reached distant points around the world. T. D. Patton, one of the students in the first class and one of the original captains, became a missionary in India in 1894 and took the game with him to that country.

One negative aspect of the rapid growth of basketball at Ys around the country was that it soon took over the facilities, crowding more established classes out of the gym. In Philadelphia, basketball was banned from the Y for a period, and teams were forced to play in dance halls and other buildings large enough to establish a court. Y officials soon realized, however, that the game's popularity would increase the Y's membership, so compromises in scheduling were achieved and basketball was once again part of the Philadelphia Y's program.

In 1896, Gulick turned over administration of the basketball rules to the Amateur Athletic Union of the United States, the administrative body for all amateur sports in the country at that time.

When Naismith came to Springfield, his intention had been to complete the training course, then return to Montreal and become a physical education director at the Y. Dr. Gulick's offer of a faculty position at the Training School changed those plans, and Naismith remained on the staff at the school until 1895, no doubt influencing many students during his years there.

One such student was W. G. Morgan, who graduated in 1894 and went to work at the Y in Holyoke, Massachusetts. He set out to invent another new game, similar to basketball but not quite as strenuous. He envisioned his new game as being suited more for older businessmen. He was successful, too, in his first year on the job, inventing a game known then as "mintonette." The game today is known as volleyball. It is not too great a stretch to call Naismith, the father of basketball, also the grandfather of volleyball.

Naismith's happiness during his Springfield years depended on factors greater than the success of basketball. He had moved into a room in the home of a widow named Mrs. Sherman, whose husband, Edwin, had recently died. The couple had 11 children, two of whom, Maude and Florence, were still living at home. Mrs. Sherman's home was near the Training School, and she began to board students as a way to produce extra income.

Another of the boarders, a man named Jim Hale, asked Maude out on a date one night. Mrs. Sherman had Florence go along as a chaperone, which prompted Hale to ask Naismith to join them. Naismith also liked Maude, and at some point during the date, Hale suggested the two change sisters so he could be with Florence. Naismith and Maude were an unlikely pair, as he was eight years older and about seven inches taller.

The two hit it off immediately, however, and even though Naismith was credited with developing the first football headgear, it was Maude Sherman who sewed the pieces of flannel together to help protect his ears. She also was attracted to Naismith's new game of basketball, and Naismith said years later that she was one of the first players on the ladies' faculty team at the Training School.

In those early days, almost as many women were playing basketball as men, although in a far different fashion. The women, starting with the Buckingham School teachers, were also among the game's most ardent fans. Naismith said their presence offered a "wholesome influence" on the game. On many occasions, however, men were not allowed to attend women's games. One of the first colleges to sponsor a women's team, Smith College, would not allow men to watch when the Smith sophomores played the freshmen because the girls were wearing bloomers.

Naismith dated Maude Sherman for more than two years before the couple became engaged. Prior to getting married, in the summer of 1893, Naismith traveled with his uncle and sister to Scotland. They spent much of the summer in and around Glasgow, visiting relatives and seeing all of the places Naismith had heard about from his grandmother. Naismith's daughter Margaret said that for years Naismith claimed one of the reasons for his trip was to buy a suit for his wedding, but her true opinion was that her father "always wanted to go and why pay for two tickets when he could see all he wanted to for the price of one. That is the Scotch for you. He knew it would take two tickets after he was married."

Naismith did bring Maude a silver pin with a scotch thistle on it, and the couple was married on June 20, 1894, at the Hope Congregational Church in Springfield. Naismith's childhood and college friend, R. Tait McKenzie, was his best man.

That marked McKenzie's second visit to see his old friend in Springfield. On the first occasion, Dr. Gulick had offered him a teaching position at the Training School, but McKenzie already was developing a strong medical practice in Montreal and declined the offer.

After the wedding, McKenzie said he didn't see any reason to worry about his old friend any longer. "Those who know him realize that he has been in good hands," McKenzie said of the new Mrs. Naismith.

Naismith's new mother-in-law was not so sure about her daughter's choice of a husband, however. Margaret Naismith recalled years later that her grandmother had been "ashamed, because Maude was marrying a redcoat," a reference to the British soldiers who had fought against the American colonies in the Revolutionary War, even though that confrontation had occurred more than a century earlier.

The couple's honeymoon consisted of riding a 22-foot sailboat on a 500-mile cruise down the Connecticut River, into Long Island Sound, around the tip of Cape Cod, and up the New England coast to Nova Scotia. Maude revealed years later that she was seasick the whole time, and she also did not take fondly to the presence of Naismith's Scottish collie dog, Roderick, who also was sick on the trip. Maude got over being seasick, but she never changed her opinion about dogs, perhaps because of what happened on the couple's return trip.

The couple had planned to take the train from Nova Scotia back to Springfield, but after Maude was settled into her seat, Naismith disappeared and was gone for several hours. Maude thought that maybe she had been deserted. When the train was almost to Springfield, however, Naismith reappeared with a big smile on his face. When Maude asked where he had been, Naismith explained that he had gone back to the baggage car to sit with Roderick because he was afraid the dog would be lonesome during the long trip.

Maude was able to forgive her husband, and the couple's first child, a daughter they named Margaret, was born on July 1, 1895, and life for the young family seemed to be idyllic.

Naismith likely could have remained on the Springfield faculty for as long as he wanted, but he soon began to think about new adventures. Dr. Gulick had a medical degree, and the pursuit of a similar degree appealed to Naismith. He had always been interested in medicine, and patching up the various injuries he saw in the gym increased his desire to attend medical school. He knew he would need a way to pay for his continuing education, and he figured that if he could get a job as a physical education director at a Y in a city with a good medical school, he could accomplish his next goal.

In the summer of 1895, Naismith found his chance when he was offered a job at the YMCA in Denver, close to the Gross Medical School. He accepted the job and was admitted to the medical school. The Denver Y was the largest branch in the United States, and the Gross Medical School, later to merge into the University of Colorado School of Medicine, had been founded in 1887 and was at that time already a well-known and highly regarded institution.

Naismith, now 33 years old and with a wife and baby daughter, was on the move again.

• • •

CHAPTER 5

A New Frontier

Moving nearly 2,000 miles in 1895 was not an easy task. For the new Mrs. Naismith, there was more involved than the physical move. Born and raised in the East, she had never lived anywhere else. She was close to her mother, and since the death of her father, that bond had grown even tighter.

Still, her love for her new husband, and the desire to see him fulfill his dreams, overrode whatever fears and apprehensions Maude Naismith had about the move west. She knew that her father, who also had been an inventor, would have approved of her marriage to Naismith and would have encouraged her to make the move west with him.

Maude's father was like her husband in at least one other way: he never made much money from his most famous invention. Edwin Sherman had invented the reaping machine, a grain harvester, but had sold the rights to the machine to Cyrus McCormick before it became famous.

After Naismith accepted the job in Denver, he and Maude decided that it would be best for him to go there alone at first—although accompanied by his pet collie—and get himself settled, into both his new job and classes at the medical school, before being joined by his wife and baby daughter. The two communicated by mail, and in a letter dated October 1, 1895, Naismith said he was ready for his wife and baby to join him. He urged them to begin their journey by train by the 15th of the month. He also described his daily schedule.

"I enjoy my studies more and more," he wrote. "My day's work is something like this: 8 A.M. physiology; 9 A.M. anatomy; 10 A.M. chemistry; 11 A.M. clinics or quiz; 12 P.M. to 1 P.M. is my office hour; 1–2 P.M. dinner; 3–3:30 office; 4–6 gym. . . . Then in evening on football field or in the gym. When am I going to have time to court my little wife? . . . I have not taken a day off nor an evening since I came, but have one reserved for my pets. I shall have every Wednesday and Sunday eves for you, my dearie." He enclosed $20 with the letter, telling his wife to "spend it as you see best."

In a return letter, Maude Naismith told her husband that Dr. Gulick had come by their house to check on her and the baby: "He said, 'Please tell the Reverend gentleman that I would like very much to hear from him.' I said I didn't know how you could study in the day for your time was so taken up, and he said, 'Well remember he learns very easily, is very quick, if it is possible for anyone to do it he will, what would be hard for most people is easy for him.'"

It was understandable that Naismith did not have time to contact his old friend and boss. In addition to his heavy school load, his work at the Y was demanding. When Naismith arrived, the Y was offering 34 classes a week in traditional educational subjects as well as in a variety of other topics that included banjo, vocal music, drawing, and first aid. More classes were soon added in art, science, foreign languages, business, and other subjects. The Y also offered weekly Bible and training sessions as well as Sunday school classes, and even conducted religious services at the jail. Naismith personally was eager to see a new group of young men begin playing basketball.

By October 20, Maude Naismith was finally prepared to begin the trip. She wrote to her husband, "I start next Tuesday without fail. I dread the journey. It seems as if I couldn't go alone but I suppose I must be brave. What other people do I can do."

The trip for Maude and the baby was eventful—she left her purse behind at one point and had to return to the train station to retrieve it—but Maude and Margaret Naismith successfully made it to Denver. Maude had been there for only two weeks when she wrote to her mother that she was terribly homesick. "When I got here I felt as if I wanted to take the first train back, and I haven't gotten over it yet. The place is beautiful, I suppose, but I can't judge until I get over being homesick. Certainly the view is just lovely, the mountains are just lovely. I have a fine view from my window, can see Pike's Peak and the whole mountain range covered with snow.

"We have been looking for a house but the houses are very small here, I mean any we could afford. I think we will have to pay $25 at least and I think that is terrible. Some of the houses have four and five rooms, only one story, they look so funny to me."

The couple finally moved into a new home while Naismith continued his busy schedule. He completed his first year of medical training in the spring of 1896 and began taking classes in such subjects as pathology, physiology, anatomy, therapeutics, and surgery.

Naismith thought his job at the Y was going well, too, but he didn't know that the Y was in serious financial trouble. The public eventually learned that the Y was in danger of closing unless it could raise $10,000. Appeals were made to church congregations across the city, and luckily there were enough donations for the Y to pay its outstanding bills and remain open. For Naismith, that meant he could continue working, going to medical school, and supporting his family.

In the summer of 1896, Maude's sister Florence came to Denver to visit. While she was there, both sisters contracted typhoid fever. Maude's illness, complicated by pneumonia, was much more serious than Florence's. Since both his mother and father had died from typhoid fever, Naismith was particularly worried about his 27-year-old wife.

One night, a nurse at the bedside realized Maude had no pulse. Thinking she was dead, the nurse called for Naismith to come quickly from another room, where he had been napping. Naismith looked at his wife's pale face, and no doubt wanting to awaken her, he reached out and slapped her. It seemed to the nurse that a miracle occurred. Maude suddenly caught a breath and moved. Her pulse returned, although faint at first, and she later regained her strength and survived.

The disease did, however, take away almost all of her hearing, leaving her virtually deaf for the rest of her life. She had to learn to communicate by reading lips.

Florence also recovered. During her visit, she fell in love with another of the medical school students. Married in the fall of 1896, they moved further west, to Butte, Montana. There, tragedy struck about a year later. Florence had a baby girl, also named Florence, but died three weeks after giving birth. James and Maude were asked to care for the baby, and they did so for the first three years of her life, until her father remarried and took the child back.

Two months after baby Florence came to live with the Naismiths, they had their own new baby, a girl named Hellen, born on December 21, 1897.

Having to care for two new babies, plus his two-year-old daughter, would have been enough to keep anybody busy without the added duties of going to medical school and working full time. The third year of medical school was the most difficult, but Naismith kept up with his class work, knowing he was getting ever closer to his goal. He didn't know that he was about to face another tragedy, one that would affect him for the rest of his life.

Naismith was in the gymnasium of the Denver Y one day, conducting a class in tumbling. One of the boys in the class attempted a somersault, but his timing was off. Instead of landing on his feet, he landed on his head. Even though he landed on a thick, padded mat, the pressure of the fall broke his neck, and he died.

The accident gave Naismith nightmares. He would jump out of bed, in a cold sweat, and find himself "shaking like a tree in a windstorm." Other nights he lay awake for hours, unable to fall asleep. He even suffered attacks during the day. The more he tried to put the accident out of his mind—and try to convince himself that it truly was an accident—the more he was unable to forget about it. He wondered if the tragedy would drive him insane.

One day, with his eyes filled with tears, Naismith went to the spot in the gymnasium where the accident had occurred and began to pray. He asked God to help alleviate his pain and suffering.

On April 8, 1898, Naismith was granted his Doctor of Medicine degree, and the school celebrated commencement four days later. He was happy he had accomplished another goal, but he did not know what further challenges awaited him. As had been the case when he graduated from the seminary but elected not to become a minister, his new medical degree did not mean that Naismith had decided to become a doctor. He was not interested in working for a hospital or entering private practice, even if these options would mean a major improvement to his financial situation. He was more interested in using his medical knowledge to further his understanding of the human body and to help develop young men into physically and mentally fit human beings. He wanted to understand not only how the human body worked, but why.

The fatal accident, however, had left him with doubts about continuing to work at the Y. It was while he was debating his future that luck, and the memory of an old friend, combined to send Naismith down a new path.

CHAPTER 6

KU Bound

Amos Alonzo Stagg had left the Training School in 1892 to become the physical education director and football coach at the University of Chicago. Stagg and Naismith remained in touch, even after Naismith moved to Denver, and Stagg knew of Naismith's graduation from medical school and readiness for a new, challenging position.

Stagg got a message one day in 1898 from his boss, William Harper, the president of the University of Chicago. Harper's counterpart at the University of Kansas, Francis Snow, had contacted Harper to see if he could make a recommendation for a job Kansas was trying to fill.

Kansas's first paid football coach, the Reverend Hector Cowan, had resigned before the beginning of the 1898 season. Cowan, a graduate of Princeton Seminary, had also served as the university's chapel director. The university hired Fielding H. Yost to become the new football coach, but he balked when told the position also included serving as the chapel director, which required him to lead the student body in prayer every morning.

Not wanting to lose Yost's services as the football coach, Snow made the decision to split up those jobs. The university, at the same time, was organizing a Department of Physical Education, and Snow added the chapel director's job to the position of head of that department. That was the position he was seeking to fill when he contacted Harper for a recommendation.

When hearing the details of the job Kansas was trying to fill, Stagg had no hesitation in making his recommendation. He fired off a telegram to Snow that read, "Recommend James Naismith, inventor of basketball, medical doctor, Presbyterian minister, tee-totaler, all-around athlete, non-smoker, and owner of vocabulary without cuss words. Address Y.M.C.A., Denver, Colorado."

It was only a matter of time before Kansas officials contacted Naismith and offered him the position. He accepted. Nowhere in his job description did the term "basketball coach" appear, because the university did not have a basketball team. For years, Naismith claimed the only reason he was offered the job was that he knew how to pray, and he might not have been far off. His salary was set at $1,300 a year, which worked out to $25 a week.

Before he, Maude, and the three girls left Denver by train in early September 1898, a woman who had cared for Margaret when Maude was ill came to say good-bye and see the family off. She also handed Naismith a package, saying it was for Margaret. She said she was worried that Margaret would not get proper food, so she was sending some with her. When the family opened the package after getting on the train, they found it contained a dozen eggs. Why, nobody ever knew. Naismith gave the eggs to the porter on the train.

When the family arrived in Lawrence, they checked into the Eldridge Hotel, and all three of the girls broke out in a rash. Margaret recalled years later that "Dad went down to Dick's Drug Store and asked Mr. Dick about a doctor. Mr. Dick directed him to a young doctor who had offices over the drug store. Dr. Jones went to the hotel to see the children. He took one good look and burst out laughing. 'If you'll take those wool shirts and stockings off the children, bathe them in cool water, the prickly heat will soon disappear and they will be all right. That may be necessary in Colorado but this Kansas heat is something else.'"

The University of Kansas had been founded in 1866, making it almost as old as the state itself, and was growing rapidly. As the one-man physical education department, Naismith was required to teach the mandatory freshman class in hygiene, the gymnastics classes, and any other classes that might be offered, to oversee the athletics department, and to lead the daily chapel service.

The service lasted for one hour in the 660-seat auditorium, with a pipe organ, inside the "new" Fraser Hall, which had opened in 1872. The service consisted of Bible reading, prayers, singing, and a message, offered either by Naismith or by a guest speaker. Even though daily service was supposed to be attended by all students, participation began to wane. That resulted in the university's changing the service to alternate days, then cutting it back further, to once a week, at 10 A.M. every Tuesday. Eventually the university withdrew the mandatory attendance rule and made chapel voluntary, before finally disbanding the service altogether.

Naismith's first office was under the stairs of Snow Hall, which housed the science building. Naismith taught his physical education classes at the same time that botany and other science classes were being conducted, and all that separated the classes was a piece of chicken wire. The "gym" was in the basement of Snow Hall, and it featured a court 36 feet wide and 84 feet long, with a line of support posts down the center of the floor. The other handicap of the facility was that it had a ceiling only 11 feet high.

At the time Naismith came to Lawrence, basketball was considered a "sissy" game. A group of women had tried to play the sport after being introduced to it by a woman named Lola Bell, who brought the game with her when she transferred from Radcliffe College in 1897. The student yearbook reported in 1899 that "A few futile attempts had been made to interest the students and faculty in the game, but without success."

So just three months after arriving in Lawrence, Naismith once again took it upon himself to educate a group of students about the virtues of the sport. He introduced the sport to his physical education classes, then organized an intramural league of eight teams, including a faculty team, though none of the players had ever played in or even seen a basketball game before. From that pool Naismith selected the members of the school's first official men's team.

Many of the players had been members of the football team. Will Sutton, a member of the Phi Beta Kappa honor society, was elected captain. One of the members of the first team was Hubert Avery, who also played football. Naismith recalled that Avery "made 1's in every subject except one, and the faculty member gave him a lower mark because he said that no man could play football and make a 1 in his class."

The first Kansas team, even though it included football players, was known more for its skill than its brawn, Naismith maintained. "These men had taken up the game more as a recreation than as an intercollegiate contest, but after playing a short time they wished to branch out and a game was scheduled with the Kansas City [YMCA] team."

On February 3, 1899, the first official men's basketball game in the history of the University of Kansas was played at the Kansas City Y. Kansas lost, 16–5. Naismith served as the referee of the game, as he often did during the early years.

"When the Kansas City team wanted the ball they went after it without respect to the rule that a player was entitled to his place on the court," Naismith later wrote. "In this way upright aggressiveness not only got the ball but injured the players. On calling fouls I was informed that no foul had been committed and it was impossible to convey the idea of it being a foul.

"My idea of sportsmanship was to play the rules as written and I kept trying to overcome this handicap with skill but we were defeated."

The school's newspaper, the *University Daily Kansan*, gave the following report of the game:

The game was called promptly at 8:45 P.M. with Kansas at the south goal. The regulation twenty minute halves were played.

After one minute of play, owing to a foul, Sutton threw a goal. The playing from this time was exceedingly fast. The YMCA after three minutes of play threw a field goal. Sutton made one of the most sensational plays of the game one minute later. The ball was thrown to him and he rolled it for three yards. [Rolling was an alternative to passing, since dribbling was still not allowed.] He was viciously beset by two YMCA men and bending backward he threw the ball fully twelve yards and got a goal.

During the next ten minutes the YMCA made a scratch goal and the half closed with the score YMCA 4, Kansas 3.

During the second half KU braced up and outplayed the YMCA. Henderson and Bowen distinguished themselves by their clever rolling and Sutton seemed to be everywhere at the same time. The latter part of this half was characterized by the number of fouls committed.

The game was finished at 9:45 P.M. Final score YMCA 16, Kansas 5. Each goal counted for one point.

A crowd of about 150 people attended the game, which also drew coverage the following day in the *Lawrence Daily Journal*. Two paragraphs on the fourth page of the four-page newspaper reported the results of the game. "The University boys always make it interesting for the enemy in any kind of a game, and last night's battle was the best seen there this season," the newspaper said. "The Tigers won for the simple and sufficient reason that they have played the game longer and are a hardier set than the Kansans."

Over the years, a variety of sources have reported that one of the players on the Kansas City team was Jesse James, identifying him as the notorious outlaw. The problem with those reports, however, is that James was shot in the head and killed in 1882, 17 years before the game. It is quite possible, however, that a Jesse James played in the first Kansas game—the son of the outlaw. The younger James would have been 23 years old, and according to census records, he was married and living in Kansas City in 1900.

In addition to lack of experience, Kansas's first squad was hampered by poor facilities. The basement in Snow Hall was inadequate for official games and barely adequate for practice because of the 11-foot-high ceiling. Naismith had to look for other venues to play "home" games. Technically, the first home game in school history was played a week later, on February 10, 1899, when the Topeka YMCA came to Lawrence, but the two teams met on the municipal skating rink.

This game had a much better result for Kansas, with the school recording the first win in its basketball history, a 31–6 triumph. William Sutton led the Kansas offense with 13 points. In its edition of February 11, 1899, the *Lawrence Daily Journal* devoted more attention to this game than it had to the one at the Y. "Perhaps fifty people were at the rink Friday evening to see the first big home game of basketball," the newspaper reported. "The gas was frozen up and after the usual throw out, the band played its old familiar air and the game began." The account also said, "The Varsity team contained men of somewhat equal size. It was evident that they had played more basketball than their opponents from the manner in which they worked together."

After five additional games that season, Kansas finished its first year of competition with a 4–3 record. Included in the victories was a 17–14 decision in a rematch against the Kansas City YMCA, in which Naismith changed the strategy and some of the players from the first game. Once again he worked as the game's referee.

"I took along the end, center and half back of the football team and the champion wrestler," Naismith wrote, "keeping in one of the regular team. These men had become interested in basketball and had played a little but were not equal to the other players in skill. The team lined up, with these men, with the instructions not to give way when the opponents pushed them but to stand their ground. The joyful expression on the faces of these men showed that they grasped the idea and the game started.

"When the Kansas City players tried to get the ball as usual, they rebounded from the football players, much to their astonishment. I called few fouls letting them play according to their own interpretation of the rules.

"It was not long until the captain of the Kansas City team asked if we were not going to call any fouls. On being told that we would gladly call fouls as we saw them, he sniffed with disgust and tried it again. It was not long until he returned. I called time and explained what they had been doing, how basketball should be played and he agreed to play the game according to the printed rules. We put in the original team and played the game."

The final game of the year was an 18–3 win over William Jewell College, the first time Kansas played a college opponent rather than a YMCA team.

Some of the visiting facilities for those early games were not much better than Snow Hall. At William Jewell, the teams played in a gym that was 18 feet wide and about 75 feet long. Though it had a high ceiling, it was lined with posts on each side. Against the Independence, Missouri, YMCA, the game was played in a loft over a livery stable, lighted by lanterns. Even the Kansas City YMCA facility had its drawbacks. It was on the third floor of the building, and one part of the court was narrower than the other, with the floor having been cut away to accommodate the stairway. One goal was fastened to the wall and the other hung between two windows.

While he was always on the lookout for men he thought could be welcome additions to the basketball team, Naismith also tried to help his friends on the football team on at least one occasion. In the fall of 1899, a freshman student caught his attention, George R. Creps, who listed his hometown as South Cedar, Kansas. Naismith thought he looked like a candidate for the football team, and he recommended him to coach Fielding Yost. Yost added him to the team, and when Kansas went to Lincoln to play the University of Nebraska, he inserted Creps into the game. Creps played a good game, helping Kansas to a victory, but then he suddenly disappeared from the team and from the campus.

His disappearance led to an investigation, and the true story eventually came out. Yost had come to Kansas from the University of West Virginia, where one of the star players was G. R. Krebs, who graduated from the school in the spring of 1899. He followed Yost to Kansas and, after changing a couple of letters in his last name, enrolled in law school. He then started "hanging around" the physical education department until he was "discovered" by Naismith. After the game, Krebs returned to West Virginia, and the only victims of the prank he and Yost had pulled off were Naismith and Nebraska.

A more serious incident occurred that fall when a student working in one of the university buildings got caught between an elevator and the floor. The top of his head was crushed. There were no hospitals in Lawrence at the time, so Naismith brought the boy to his house and performed surgery on the family's dining room table. At his wife's urging, a neighbor, Mrs. Hattan, allowed the boy to move into her house, and she continued to care for him until he recovered.

The following seasons of Kansas basketball differed little from the first year, with Naismith devoting far more attention to his teaching duties and his work as the chapel leader than to coaching the team. The aspect of the sport that concerned him most was the inadequate playing facilities, which worsened when a fire destroyed the Armory that housed the skating rink.

Naismith spent the summer of 1900 working as an instructor at Ottawa College in nearby Ottawa, Kansas, earning an extra $100 for three weeks of work, and as an instructor at the YMCA camp for boys in Lake Geneva, Wisconsin. That same year, his niece Florence was reunited with her father after he remarried, and James and Maude welcomed their third child, John, who was born in November. Though John was a traditional Naismith name, the boy was always known as Jack instead.

The family was now established in Lawrence, having joined the First Presbyterian Church, where Naismith began teaching an adult Sunday school class. The lessons became so popular that members of other churches began to come as well, but those people did not stay for the church service, irritating the church officials. Naismith decided to rent a room in a nearby mortuary, where for several years he conducted the classes for anyone who wanted to come. Naismith later taught a class for high school boys, and that proved so popular that when the boys graduated from high school, they continued to come to Naismith's class, refusing to move up to the adult class.

His family and his teaching, whether it was on Sunday or during the week at the university, were obviously Naismith's passion and his priorities. He taught the required freshman hygiene course, a class in kinesiology, and courses in fencing and gymnastics. "One of Dr. Naismith's strong points as a teacher was to challenge his students with questions, often resulting in heated arguments in class," wrote Jack Hammig, in a master's thesis on Naismith at Kansas in 1962. "He considered a well conceived argument as a sound teaching device."

It was considered hard to interest the students in the hygiene class, which met once a week at 4:30 in the afternoon, a time when most students were tired and wanted to be finished with classes for the day. Students knew there was little change in the course material from year to year, so they devised ways to evade the mandatory attendance rule, with one student answering "present" for several of his missing friends. Naismith no doubt knew what was going on, but he never let on.

He was more interested in working with the students who were there, and who wanted to learn. He also enjoyed counseling and mentoring students, and was always willing to offer any kind of assistance that was needed. He quickly became one of the more popular professors on campus.

During his physical education classes, Naismith continued to try to invent new games to keep his students interested. None of his new inventions—named war-tug, hy-lo ball, and vrille—ever caught on to the degree that basketball did. He also brought additional sports to the school—introducing rowing and overseeing the construction of a golf course on campus—as well as teaching lacrosse and becoming the school's first track coach.

In the summer of 1901, Naismith took his family with him to the YMCA camp in Wisconsin to escape the wicked Kansas heat. Maude's mother met the family in Chicago and then returned to Lawrence to live with her daughter's family.

Kansas won just four of its 12 basketball games in the 1900–1901 season, and Naismith realized that other schools were learning more about the game with each passing year. It was during a game against Haskell Institute that season that he witnessed first hand one of the changes in the game—a zone defense.

Until that time, every school that Kansas had played used a strict man-to-man defense. One player was assigned to guard a player on the opposing team, and it was his responsibility to stay with him no matter where he went on the court, with the main objective being to keep him from scoring.

"Haskell had a player, Archiquette, who had learned to play the guard position at Carlisle, one of the first institutions to take up the game, and was known as one of the best guards in the country," Naismith wrote. "Few goals were made by his opposing forward because of his ability to play the man-to-man defense.

"Kansas had a forward, Fred Owens, who was as expert at eluding the opposing guard as Archiquette was at intercepting forwards. Owens was a good shot at goal and was depended on to make most of the points for his team. In the first game . . . Archiquette was told to follow Owens and so well did he do this that Owens made very few tries for goal and as Owens was unable to make his usual quota Kansas was defeated."

In the second game, Kansas moved Owens to guard and played another speedy player at forward. When Archiquette found Owens scoring at will, he changed strategy at halftime and started guarding both players by defending an area rather than one individual—the first known zone defense.

Kansas's record was slightly improved the following seasons, as the team went 5–7 in 1901–1902 and 7–8 in 1902–1903. The team's biggest problem was the lack of an adequate facility for home games, which usually had to be played at the Lawrence YMCA. It was still true that Naismith viewed the sport more as a recreational activity than a competitive activity, which is why, especially when Kansas was on the road, he spent more time working as the referee of the game than he did coaching his players. He was always much more interested in their total development physically, and mentally, than in whether the team won or lost a particular game. He was also still concerned with the growth of basketball and worked hard to promote the game wherever possible.

One student who came under Naismith's guidance in those years was a man named A. A. Whipple, who arrived at KU in 1903. Naismith recalled the day when Whipple came up to him in the gym "with tears in his eyes and discouragement in his heart."

"He had come to the university with the ambition of making the football team," Naismith wrote. "When he appeared on the field the coaches told him to turn in his suit and not to come on the field again. He was about 6 feet tall and weighed about 118 pounds and I did not blame the coaches. I found out later that his father had sent him up to the university not so much for his educational advancement as for his physical development. He had a cleft palate and hare lip. His uncle had the same condition and his father thought that by taking part in exercise it might eliminate that defect. It seemed to the boy that his whole scheme of life was gone.

"I pointed out to him that there were other forms of athletics in which he could participate that would help him. He returned in a few days and I was able to point out to him some of the track events that would give him the physical development and at which he might excel. Before he left school he was captain of the track team and held the record in the pole vault, high jump, high hurdles and the shot put."

Even more important to Naismith than his students were his wife and children. When the family did not accompany him back to Wisconsin in the summer of 1902, he wrote to Maude frequently and almost always talked about how much he missed being home with them.

"My own dearie," he wrote in a letter dated July 19, 1902. "Your sweet letter came today and I was just delighted and have read it over a couple of times and it seems sweeter each time. Your love is very precious to me and you are just as precious as you can be to your old sweetheart. How I do love you. We are surrounded here with bridal couples. There is one in our tent and a couple next door. They think that love rises and sets in their little circle but I know that honeymoon love is only the beginning of good things. Our love today is of that enduring kind that has been tested and has stood the strains. I have thought several times of the time when I nearly lost you and the thought of losing you is so horrible that I cannot think of it. I feel sure that God has some work for us to do and that He will help enable us to do it."

After he returned to Lawrence in the fall, Naismith was in the Snow Hall basement one day when he noticed the janitor, Mr. Crocker, go through a hole in the floor. Investigating further, Naismith discovered that there was about five feet of space between the basement floor and the actual foundation of the building. He was successful in persuading school officials to remove the floor and lower it to the foundation, making the ceiling 16 feet high instead of 11, much more adequate for playing basketball.

Nothing could be done about the support posts that ran down the middle of the gymnasium floor, however, and many teams refused to play games there for fear their players could be seriously injured. Naismith began to lobby hard for the construction of a new gymnasium, and Frank Strong, who had replaced Snow as chancellor in 1902, agreed that it was a reasonable request. Planning began on the new Robinson Gymnasium.

Heavy spring rains in 1903 forced the Kaw River out of its banks and flooded an area in north Lawrence. When Naismith heard men were being asked to go across the swollen river to rescue stranded residents, he did not hesitate to volunteer. One family was stuck on its roof with a sick girl.

"My father, being a doctor and having handled boats all his life, volunteered to go cross and take some medicine and do what he could," Hellen Naismith wrote years later. "Another man volunteered to go with him. They left the landing with another boat. When they hit mid-stream a log hit the boat and it turned over. They were too close to the dam to do anything and the boat and the two men in it went over. The report was that Dad had drowned.

"Some one on the south shore went to the Presbyterian minister and told him what had happened and asked him to go to the house and tell my mother. It was in the middle of the morning when he came to the front door to tell her. In a very short time all the neighbors and many friends were there too. In the afternoon there was a steady stream of people, and the house was full, all come to express their sympathy, when in walked my father.

"His clothes were covered with mud, he had on hip boots and they were dripping all over the floor. I'm not sure who was more surprised, my father or his friends. After much explaining the story was finally told. It was the other boat which tipped over and only one of the men had been saved, but, my father was safe. The men had lowered the girl, who was ill, into the boat and brought her back to the south side where she was being taken care of. For many years after that her mother and father would bring fresh vegetables and chickens to my folks every week or two."

Mrs. Sherman's health was failing, and she wanted to return to her home in Springfield. Naismith took her there in the summer of 1904, and word came shortly before Thanksgiving that she had died. That came a month after the Naismith's fourth child, a girl named Maude Ann, was born. She weighed less than four pounds at birth, and it was several days before the Naismiths knew she would live.

Ever since the family had moved to Lawrence, the children had been cared for by Auntie Silvers, who, Hellen said, "could tell the most fascinating stories I have ever heard and could keep us all quiet for hours at a time. Her stories were never told the same any two times." Even though Auntie Silvers was black, the Naismiths treated her like a member of their family and never considered her a slave or maid. Naismith felt strongly about how women should be treated, black or white, again no doubt thinking about his own childhood and how much he revered his own mother, both when she was alive and after she died.

It was in the fall of 1903 that Naismith got involved with helping the first Kansas women's basketball team. Mary Bennett was the coach, but after the team lost its first two games, Naismith was asked to assist Bennett. The team won its last six games.

One of the issues with the team, as it had been for some of the East Coast women's teams the previous few seasons, was whether male spectators should be allowed to watch the games. With some reluctance, KU officials decided to admit men who were specifically invited. "These tickets are not offered for promiscuous public sale. . . . If you are approached by a damsel and coyly solicited to make a purchase, you are to consider the invitation a personal compliment," a school announcement said.

The men's team continued to perform about the same as it had ever since Naismith had introduced the game to Kansas, going 5–8 in the 1903–1904 season. There was hope on the horizon, however, although neither Naismith nor anyone else really knew it at the time.

The captain of that year's team was Harry "Pete" Allen, who had come to Kansas from Independence, Missouri, originally to play tackle on the football team. He turned out to be one of the school's finest all-around athletes in the early years of the century, also becoming a pitcher on the school's baseball team in addition to being named the captain of the basketball team.

Basketball was the sport of choice of Allen's younger brother, Forrest, and he frequently made the trip from Independence to Lawrence to watch his older brother play. Forrest was a member of the Kansas City Athletic Club, an Amateur Athletic Union (AAU) team that beat Kansas 27–10 on February 18, 1904.

The AAU had sponsored a national championship in basketball as early as 1897, drawing mostly local teams from New York, but because the sport was spreading rapidly, the 1901 championship was won by a team from Chicago. There was no national tournament in 1902 or 1903, but the team generally regarded as the best in the country was the Buffalo Germans from the YMCA in Buffalo, New York. Led by Forrest Allen, the Kansas City club invited the Germans to come and play a three-game series in the spring of 1905.

Naismith was in attendance as the two teams split the first two games. After each game, the losing side naturally complained about the officiating, and both sides asked Naismith to referee the third and deciding game. Naismith agreed, but warned both teams before the game that it would be played by his rules. It was well known that Naismith did not appreciate rough or overly aggressive play. His selection as the referee was a tremendous compliment to Naismith's sense of fair play and integrity.

The Kansas City players, having had more experience with Naismith during their games against Kansas, knew what to expect. "Games in which he officiated generally went off smoothly, for he knew the game, and the players took his word as final," said Tom

Shiras, a member of the Kansas City team, years later. "His regulation uniform when acting as an official in a game was a dark, tight woolen jersey and a cap."

The game drew a crowd of 4,000 fans, and the Kansas City team won easily, 45–14. The rules of the day called for one player to take all of his team's free throws, and the player who did that for Kansas City was Forrest Allen, making 17 of his attempts.

The Buffalo Germans were more upset by the way the game was called by Naismith, with their team captain, a man named Heerdt, quoted as saying, "It's a baby game the way it was played."

Naismith said his work as the referee prevented him from watching the individual players and their performance, but he already knew about Allen from his older brother. Even though he had never graduated from high school, Forrest Allen was planning on attending college in the fall of 1905, and his decision was between the universities of Kansas and Missouri.

In a 1967 interview, Allen explained why he picked Kansas, his brother's school. "I came out there to see those games and naturally became interested in the University of Kansas. I noticed that Lawrence had wide, paved streets. Columbia had muddy streets. They hadn't lifted Missouri out of the mud then. The store fronts were different. Lawrence had all glass fronts and the merchants were very progressive in appearance, while Columbia had many of their store fronts boarded up. I could see the difference, and I wanted to go to a place that was progressive."

In the fall of 1905, Forrest Allen set foot on the Kansas campus, two months before his twentieth birthday, with the intention of becoming a lawyer. Those plans soon changed.

CHAPTER 7

• • •

The Student Arrives

Allen's arrival on the Kansas campus was big news, and there was more anticipation about the upcoming basketball season than ever before. On October 18, the *University Daily Kansan* reported that Allen had made his first appearance on the Snow Hall court the previous night.

"The ceiling was too low for him to show how well he could throw long goals, but he gave the men some good ideas of how to get into the game," the newspaper reported. "Allen will be able to play in the games on this year's schedule, and will make a strong addition to the team. He is one of the world's champions and is said to be the best goal thrower in the world."

Though not yet affiliated with an official conference, Kansas agreed to follow the rules of the Chicago Conference, the precursor to the Big Ten, during the 1905–1906 season. One of the rules of the conference was that freshman were not eligible to play on the varsity during the first semester, so Allen and another freshman, Tommy Johnson, helped form the school's first freshman team. The team played the varsity three times, winning once.

There were no rules about playing for AAU teams at the same time a player was on a college team, so Allen played for the Kansas City Athletic Club team that fall, and also over Christmas for the Modern Woodmen team of Independence.

The day Naismith, the rest of the team, and all Kansas basketball fans were awaiting, however, was February 8, 1906, when Allen became eligible to join the Kansas varsity. He came off the bench in the second half, helping Kansas to a 40–10 win over the Wyandotte Athletic Club. He had the same role the following day, in a 43–16 Kansas victory over the Independence Athletic Club.

Allen's first start for Kansas came on February 12, in Lincoln against the University of Nebraska. He scored 23 points, leading Kansas to a 37–17 triumph. His best game was also the last game of the season, at home against the school now known as Emporia State. Allen scored 26 points, a school record that would stand until 1915, to power Kansas to a 60–13 win.

Kansas finished the season with a 12–7 record, the first and only time during Naismith's coaching tenure that the squad had a winning record for the year. The last two home games were played before packed stands at Snow Hall. Allen's importance to the team was so great that the final scheduled game of the year, against Baker, was called off when it was determined that Allen would not be able to play because of an injured hand. In its review of the season, the *University Daily Kansan* said of Allen, "He is a steady, consistent player who can be depended upon to do all that is possible for the best interests of the team and the university."

Naismith was pleased with the year's results, not only because he knew a winning record made his players feel better, but because he thought the success of the team would translate into greater attendance at the games and aid the construction of the new Robinson Gym. Naismith wanted the gym for more than just its ability to accommodate the basketball team, of course. It would give him more room for all of his physical education classes and other sports activities, which still held more personal interest for him than did the basketball team.

Like his older brother, Allen proved to be more than a one-sport star. He had played football in the fall, and when the basketball season was over, Allen joined the school's baseball team, being used as a pitcher and an infielder. Basketball was clearly his priority, however. In addition to playing for Kansas, Allen had been involved with the Baker basketball team that season. Located just 20 miles south of Lawrence in Baldwin City, Baker did not have a coach, and after making inquiries, the school officials asked Allen to work with the team on a part-time basis.

Legend has recorded a story, which may or may not be true, about what happened when Allen was set to return to Kansas for his sophomore year in the fall of 1906. According to the story, the officials at Baker, impressed with Allen's work with their team the previous season, wrote to Kansas and offered him the job of coaching their team in the upcoming season. The letter made its way to Naismith, who reportedly called Allen to his office.

"I've got a good joke for you, you bloody beggar," Naismith reportedly told Allen. "They want you to coach basketball down at Baker."

"What's so funny about that?" Allen said.

"Why, you can't coach basketball, you just play it," Naismith replied.

Did that meeting actually happen, with the dialogue as history has recorded? It is impossible to say. Naismith did not mention the letter, the meeting, or the exchange with Allen in any of his autobiographical notes. In a biography of Allen, *Phog Allen: The Father of Basketball Coaching*, author Blair Kerkhoff suggests that the story might have been exaggerated over the years.

Kerkhoff reports that Allen probably received the offer to coach Baker from school officials in the fall of 1905, after they learned of his success with the Kansas City club in the game against Buffalo. Once he had success coaching part time at Baker, it was only natural for them to want him to continue to coach. Yet, according to Kerkhoff, Allen repeated the story of his meeting and conversation with Naismith in many speeches and articles, and never made reference to having already received an offer from Baker a year earlier.

Whatever its truth, history has recorded that exchange, and its final line—"You can't coach basketball, you just play it"— has become one of Naismith's most famous quotes. Whether he made that statement to Allen or not, there is no question that the quote accurately described Naismith's opinion about the importance and value of a coach in his invented sport.

And whether or not the meeting actually occurred, it is known that Allen left Kansas to accept the Baker job, ending his playing career in Lawrence after one season.

After confirming that Allen was leaving, Naismith called a team meeting in his office and broke the news to Allen's former teammates. The team had been counting on Allen to lead them again in the 1906–07 season, having already elected him team captain for the upcoming year despite his standing as only a sophomore.

Allen's departure greatly affected the team, which limped to another losing season, finishing the year with a 7–8 record. One of the losses was to Allen's Baker team, 39–24. After the game, the *University Daily Kansan* reported what many others had begun to realize. With Naismith working as the director of physical education, teaching classes, and still leading the chapel service, he had little time to work with the school's basketball team, even if he thought there was some value to coaching. He did make up the team's schedule, but rarely traveled to away games, and when he did, he often worked as the referee rather than as Kansas's coach. "The great difficulties in developing a team are the lack of suitable quarters in which to train and the lack of a coach," the *Kansan* said. "Dr. James Naismith, the inventor of the game, is so busy with his work as athletic director that he rarely finds time to give the men thorough training."

Allen had kept in touch with the Kansas players, having come to Lawrence at least twice during the season to work with them at practices. Naismith also started to realize that he was spreading himself too thin. After the 1907 season, Naismith agreed to step down as the school's basketball coach. He was promoted from the rank of associate professor to a full professorship and placed in charge of the final details of the construction of the new Robinson Gym.

Naismith's basketball coaching career was over. In nine seasons, his teams combined for a 55–60 record. To date he remains the only coach in Kansas history with a losing career record.

The move away from coaching did not upset Naismith. To the contrary, it probably gave him added pleasure because it allowed him to concentrate on activities that he thought were more important than basketball. One of his proudest moments came during the opening of the new Robinson Gymnasium, modeled on the YMCA in Springfield, Massachusetts. The facility, which had cost $100,000 to build, immediately became the best athletic facility west of the Mississippi River. Located in the gym's basement were 1,500 lockers for men and women; the building included a swimming pool, a training area for the football team, room for the rest of the physical education classes and activities, and a full-size basketball facility, with a high ceiling, no posts down the middle of the court, and room for 3,000 spectators.

The Kansas team played its first game in the new gym on December 13, 1907, against Ottawa and won easily, 66–22. General admission seats cost 25 cents, and reserved seats were 10 cents extra. It was the first Kansas game under the new coach, Forrest Allen, who was now being referred to more and more by the nickname that would stay with him the rest of his life, Phog Allen.

Naismith had turned the team over to Allen, at the same time overseeing Kansas's move into the new Missouri Valley Conference, joining the universities of Missouri, Nebraska, Iowa, and Washington University of St. Louis. Allen also continued to coach at Baker for a final year, but thanks to good train service between Kansas City, Lawrence, and Baldwin City, still had enough time to guide Kansas to an 18–6 record, including a perfect 6–0 mark in the league, winning the first conference championship.

Relinquishing the basketball coaching assignment gave Naismith more time to pursue other activities, which he enjoyed more. It has been documented that Naismith actually played basketball—the game he invented—only twice, once at Springfield and once more at Kansas, in an 1898 game.

"I guess my early training in wrestling, boxing and football was too much for me," he said. "My reflexes made me hold my opponents. So I have sympathy for boys who make inadvertent fouls, but I cannot stand deliberate ones."

Some of the sports that Naismith enjoyed more than basketball, and which he either brought to Kansas or helped develop, included wrestling, fencing, lacrosse, golf, track and field, and rowing. Definitely a visionary, he was not consumed by basketball, and he never pursued the fame or fortune that the sport could have provided him. He had other goals in his life.

When he arrived at Kansas, he found the university had purchased the entire inventory of a defunct gymnasium in Atchison, Kansas, two years earlier, including a variety of fencing equipment. Nobody at the school knew how to use any of it until Naismith arrived in Lawrence.

He originated the idea of building a golf course on the campus, near where the football stadium now is located, and volunteered to give students, faculty members, and Lawrence residents lessons. The game proved to be so popular that the school administration had to pass a regulation closing the course on Sundays.

Interest in track and field events also flourished under Naismith, so much so that the school had to add an assistant for him to help coach the team, Fay Moulton, the first KU athlete to participate in the Olympics. By 1907 Kansas had a full-time track coach, working under Naismith's guidance.

Naismith had played lacrosse growing up in Canada, and always considered it one of his favorite sports, so it was natural that he introduced it to the Kansas students. The game became popular enough that in the school's 1908 yearbook, the lacrosse team photo received the same treatment as the photo of the men's basketball team.

As important as it was for him to develop those teams and prepare them for competition against other universities, Naismith was proud of his work in bringing intramural athletics to the university, so that students who otherwise might not have participated in athletics got to compete. Naismith, through his own education, considered athletic competition a true component of a student's overall development at the university, and the intramural program let those students receive the benefits of physical activity.

His work with students interested in rowing began as an intramural activity. The first regatta on the Kaw River in 1908 drew 71 entries and a large crowd of spectators. When Potter Lake was built on campus—originally with the idea that the water could be used in case of fire at a university building—it quickly became a favorite spot for the students to swim and canoe. The university's annual canoe regatta was soon being held at the lake.

Naismith and his family moved to a new house with a larger yard, where the growing children had more space to play. Whenever Naismith went out of town on a trip, he always returned with a gift for his wife and for one of the children. "Once it was a violin, another time a set of furs but always something nice," Hellen Naismith recalled. "We always knew before he went who was the lucky one and if our requests were not too outlandish we usually got what we asked for."

Naismith no doubt always remembered those presents, but on a trip to New York, in 1908, he wrote to his wife that he had forgotten one thing when his train arrived in Pittsburgh, where he had to change trains. "I got ready to leave at 4:45," he wrote. "Just at four the clocks struck five and my train was gone. I had forgotten to change from Central to Eastern time. But it was all right. . . . I caught the next train and got to Philadelphia only 15 minutes behind the other."

Holidays were also an enjoyable time around the Naismith house. Hellen Naismith recalled one Fourth of July and one Memorial Day in particular during her early childhood:

It was a hot Fourth of July night as only Kansas can have. All of the children from the neighborhood, and many of their parents, had gathered at our house to watch the display of fireworks. It was early in the century and fireworks were the order of the day. All contributed their share and the clothes basket was filled to overflowing with roman candles, skyrockets, pin wheels, little firecrackers, giant crackers, harmless ones and dangerous ones. The children were restless and tired, the parents were cross and tired, but this was the moment the children had waited for all that long, hot day.

The moment had arrived. My father, a large broad shouldered man, his hair parted in the middle, giving him a rather scholarly look and a large bristling moustache which gave him a rather fierce look, picked a pin wheel out of the basket, walked over to one of the large elms that lined the sidewalk and slipped the pin wheel over a nail that had been driven into the tree just before dinner. It seemed to the impatient children as though the wick would never burn. Eventually it did and the sparks flew. The wheel did not turn and the sparks flew directly into the basket. First there was a sputter, then a flash and finally all of the glory of the Fourth burst forth as skyrockets and roman candles shot in every direction. Firecrackers popped and boomed. Our evening's entertainment was over all too soon.

Memorial Day was also a day for family observances, Hellen Naismith said:

Those who had not picked their flowers the night before were out early gathering great baskets of flowers before the sun came up. Maude Ann was downstairs and had picked every flower in the garden before anyone else was awake. Her teacher had been telling the class stories about Decoration Day. She had explained to them the significance of the day, and how it started, and how it had grown into a national holiday.

The breakfast was on the table, the blessing had been said when Maude Ann stated, "Daddy, I'm ready, When can we go?" That question was asked over and over, not only at breakfast but every few minutes during the morning. Finally in desperation he sat down on the porch steps and undertook to explain that the family had no graves to decorate and how fortunate they were.

Maude Ann flung her arms around his neck and burst out crying. "But Daddy I want a grave to decorate. All the others will decorate graves and I won't." She was a heartbroken little girl. She wouldn't have anything to tell the class when she went back and everyone else would.

When her father finally realized how very important it was to her he told her to stop crying and to run tell her mother to dress her and he would see what he could do about it. It wasn't long until they were starting for the cemetery . . . a father trying to make life worth living for a little girl and a happy little girl carrying a basket of half wilted flowers. She was able to tell the class the next day that she and her Daddy found a grave with only a small American flag on it and they decorated it with flowers.

When he wasn't spending that quality time with his family, Naismith could usually be found in his office in new Robinson Gym, or off in a corner teaching fencing to a small group of students, or teaching one of his other classes.

What he wasn't doing, however, was worrying about the fate of the school's basketball team. Naismith had put that assignment firmly in Allen's hands, and he never stopped in at Allen's office to offer advice. He did attend the games when he was in town, but he always sat quietly in his seat, observing the action, without cheering or displaying any other signs of emotion.

Allen, despite being about the same age as most of the players, quickly demonstrated his coaching ability. He followed up his first year as Kansas's coach by leading the team to a 25–3 record in the 1908–1909 season, including an 8–2 conference mark and a second consecutive league title.

Allen, who had come to Kansas with the intention of becoming a lawyer, had learned at least one other thing from Naismith. He saw that if he intended to remain in coaching, it would be wise to have some kind of medical training. He decided to leave Kansas in 1909 to begin training as an osteopath at the Central College of Osteopathy in Kansas City.

Naismith, having always believed in and supported the pursuit of additional education, no doubt was pleased with Allen's decision. It meant, however, that he had to hire another coach for the basketball team. The job went to William O. Hamilton, who had been coaching a high school team in Kansas City. Hamilton had gone to William Jewell College in suburban Kansas City, where he both played and coached the team while a student.

Hamilton would remain at Kansas for a decade, and while he enjoyed success, Naismith began to voice his displeasure about some of the changes that were beginning to occur in "his" game. Specifically, Naismith was concerned about how rough the game was getting. During a 1910 game against rival Missouri, a particularly physical game, Naismith remarked, "Oh my gracious, they are murdering my game."

As a member of the national rules committee, Naismith led the call for officials to more closely enforce the rules of the game, particularly the "no physical contact" rule. He could tell from watching the Kansas games that many players believed that rough and physical play was a way to overcome a team with more skilled players.

The situation was even worse, Naismith found out from friends and associates, in games played in the East. There, coaches would get together before a game and agree to waive the rule that called for players to be removed from the game after they had committed four personal fouls. In one such game, more than 40 fouls were called—on each team—and only three field goals were made. The rest of the points came on free throws, making for a long and boring game for the fans in attendance.

The rules committee believed that simply enforcing the rules would make a difference in the quality of the play and once again produce the desired effect of emphasizing the skills of the players. "Under this new style of playing the ideal player will be the fast player who can beat his man to the ball," the rules committee said. "The team that plays the man and not the ball will be handicapped as they will be continually fouling, while the side that plays the ball and relies on their ability to beat their opponents to the ball will make very few fouls and in addition will be able to play faster ball than their opponents."

Another area that was becoming a greater concern for Naismith was what he termed "commercialism in sports." In an address later reprinted in the May 1911 issue of *The Graduate Magazine* of the University of Kansas, Naismith listed 16 reasons why commercialism would have a negative impact on athletics in colleges and universities. Included in his reasons were that commercialism puts sports "in a wrong perspective for the individual who is preparing himself for his life work," "it tends to over-specialization and leads to over-training," "it makes work of sport," "it puts too much stress on the winning of the game," "it leads to a worship of the dollar in the field of athletics," "it stimulates betting," "it leads to a class distinction," "it makes sport a spectacle rather than a source of recreation," and "it destroys class spirit and college loyalty." Further, "athletics have an educational value and this should be their aim in an educational institution."

Another reason cited by Naismith was that "athletics may be a great moral factor. This phase of the subject is leading to the playground movement. Athletics and the playgrounds furnish the laboratory in which the great moral lessons of fair play and the square deal are being taught to children."

Finally, he noted that "the college student is the hero of the high school boy. It is the duty of every student to align himself with the highest and most advanced ideals of sports as well as of everything else. The Amateur Athletic Union has stood for clean sport, and it is their boast that but for them sport would have perished. The Union has come to the point where they are willing to recognize the amateur standing of the colleges and their code of eligibility. We cannot at this time make a backward movement."

Given the current situation in all organized sports, Naismith's remarks are even more valid nearly 100 years after his 1911 speech.

By this point, Naismith was devoting much of his time to the study of athletes and students in general, beginning at a very early age. Much of his interest stemmed from his medical school training. On April 6, 1907, the *Lawrence Daily Journal* ran a story about one of Naismith's research projects under the headline, "Is Working on Shorties; Dr. Naismith has machine to make people taller."

In the article, Naismith described experiments in which he was attempting to determine whether a man could be made to grow tall, in part by using a "stretching" machine he had invented. "The theory of my experiments," the newspaper quoted Naismith as saying, "is one which has been advanced by physicians for the last four years, that the body is more or less elastic and that by a correct stretching system it can be made to lengthen. It is claimed that by stretching the body 30 minutes a day for six months it will lengthen two inches. Not only the lower limbs and spinal column can be stretched, but also the neck and arms may be made [longer] in proportion with the rest of the body. I am conducting the experiments to see if the claims of firms manufacturing stretching machines are justifiable."

Naismith said he believed that the best time to "stretch" individuals was when they were between five months and one year of age. The newspaper said Naismith believed that five minutes of stretching in the evening might cause a baby to grow as much as resting overnight. The danger, Naismith told the newspaper, was that a patient might grow too fast and that there was no way to stop it.

It is unknown how long Naismith conducted the tests, and what final results he achieved, but his personal records did contain volumes of statistics that he dutifully recorded over the years during his physical examinations of freshmen students at the university. He kept track of measurements such as height, weight, girth of each arm, girth of chest, girth of legs, and even the average hours of sleep a student obtained per night, as well as how many hours he spent each day in the open air. That kind of information fascinated Naismith, who earlier in his career had witnessed Dr. Gulick in Springfield collecting much of the same data.

Another area of study for Naismith that attracted a great deal of attention was his invention of a crude breathalyzer, designed to test the effects of alcohol on the nervous system. He took a rod about a quarter-inch in diameter and asked people who had been drinking to try to insert it into a hole approximately a half-inch in diameter in the center of a metal block. Anybody who hit the block would set off an electrical circuit, and the information was recorded on a revolving drum. Naismith's belief was that the more alcohol a person had consumed, the harder it would be for him to place the rod in the hole correctly.

He asked professors in the pharmacy lab to prepare samples of alcohol and a control beverage, and he asked students to line up in Robinson Gymnasium so that he could administer the tests and record the results. When he could not get enough students to participate, he performed the tests on himself.

Only once did Maude Naismith get upset with her husband's devotion to conducting medical tests. After the couple's fifth and final child was born, a son named James Sherman, on May 7, 1913, Naismith brought the baby to his child development class when the child was only three days old. During his lecture, he marked the baby in red and blue chalk to emphasize points he was making. Naismith forgot to wash off the chalk marks before taking the baby back home to his mother, who stated emphatically, "I'll lend no more of my babies" to such lectures, studies, and experiments.

Naismith always was interested in learning more, doing more, trying to keep pace with the changes in the world, and preparing himself for the next challenge that awaited him. A war was brewing in Europe, and that concerned Naismith a great deal. Years before, when he graduated from the seminary at McGill, he was not ordained as a minister because he decided to go to the YMCA Training School in Springfield instead of pursuing a pastorate. Now, in 1916, when he was 54 years old, he finally obtained his ordination.

His main reason for becoming ordained was to qualify as a chaplain in the United States Army, even though he was officially a Canadian citizen. He joined the Kansas National Guard, was appointed as a chaplain, and was given the rank of captain.

In addition to the deteriorating situation in Europe, a crisis was developing along the border between the United States and Mexico. Pancho Villa was leading a revolution, which was about to capture Naismith's full attention.

CHAPTER 8

A Revolution Calls

Pancho Villa was a hero to the poor people of Mexico, and he had counted on support from the United States in his attempt to become the president of the country in 1915. When the U.S. government instead recognized the new Mexican government, Villa became upset. He took revenge on the United States by leading his troops on raids that killed many Americans along the border.

Concerned for the safety of Americans in the area, President Wilson ordered U.S. troops, under the command of General John J. "Black Jack" Pershing, to Texas and New Mexico, where they began patrolling the border. The arrival of U.S. troops did temporarily dissuade Villa from making raids into U.S. territory, but he continued to kill Americans who traveled into Mexico, including 17 mining engineers from Texas who had been invited by the Mexican government to reopen mines in the country.

Two months later, Villa and 500 troops attacked the U.S. Cavalry camp at Columbus, New Mexico, killing 14 American soldiers and 10 civilians. He had now gotten the attention of the U.S. government. President Wilson called out 15,000 militia members and stationed them along the U.S. border with Mexico. He also authorized Pershing to lead an expeditionary force into Mexico to capture Villa.

While Pershing's troops were in Mexico, National Guard units from several states, including Kansas, were dispatched to secure the border. On June 20, 1916, Captain James Naismith received a telegram from the adjutant general of the Kansas National Guard: "Report for mobilization at Fort Riley Friday June 23. Orders to your command have been issued."

Naismith did not wait until the 23rd; he immediately left Lawrence and headed west to Fort Riley. He left so quickly, in fact, that he forgot to take his teeth with him and had to write home to ask his wife or daughter to send them as quickly as possible. Within two weeks, Naismith and the rest of the First Regiment were on a train, headed south toward the border between Texas and Mexico.

It was hard for Maude Naismith and the couple's children to watch him leave. The family was already in the middle of one crisis, as the oldest daughter, Margaret, had eloped and married George Stanley after completing only two years of her education at the University of Kansas. With her father gone, the next oldest daughter, Hellen, helped her mother take care of the younger children, dropping out of school for a year.

After Naismith left, his oldest son, Jack, decided he wanted to follow in his dad's footsteps and become a soldier too. The 15-year-old boy left Lawrence and reached the small town of St. Mary's, Kansas, where he stopped for the night, sleeping in a park. That turned out to be the same night that a safe in the St. Mary's State Bank was blown up and a thief escaped with $2,400. The police picked Jack up in the park, believing he might be the culprit, and kept him for questioning for several hours before a family friend was able to identify him and gain his release.

Captain Naismith knew none of that when he arrived at his assigned post at Eagle Pass, Texas, along the Rio Grande River, across the border from the Mexican town of Piedras Negras, and immediately went to work. In one of his first letters home to his wife, dated July 12, he described what he was doing and how he was adjusting to Army life. "I am feeling like a fighting cock and feel more at home. Most of my time has been taken up with talking to young men who have families and want to go home. I am writing to men in their home towns to have them take care of the wives. . . . I am trying to do my work cheerfully and I want you to look on the bright side for a few more days, and the sun will come out from behind the clouds. Tell me how to cheer up the poor fellows who are in worse circumstances than I am. . . . It hurts me to have you worried."

In another letter a couple of weeks later, Naismith described one counseling session he had with another soldier. "I am learning something about Army life and a little about life in general. I read a young man's letter last night from his wife. She accused him of having a little Mexican and nearly broke the heart of the poor boy. He cried nearly all night. It was a letter from a young wife who is in a condition new to her, and she wrote what she and many another girl has felt at such a time. I told him that she was sorry about it before the letter had left her home town."

Just a couple of weeks into his assignment, Naismith knew what his biggest challenges were going to be—trying to teach the Army men to stay away from the houses of prostitution that flourished around military camps, and coming up with alternative forms of entertainment to keep them occupied and satisfied during their free time. These challenges would stay with Naismith all through his time on the Mexican border, and even after he went overseas, to France, where he stayed for almost two years.

Some of the resistance against Naismith's efforts came from fellow Army officers, which somewhat surprised him. "We have succeeded in closing up the house [of prostitution] before it ever got started," Naismith wrote in a letter to Maude on July 30. "I do not anticipate for a moment that they will not make another effort but they will be careful.

"Sentiment is in our favor now, but it looked dark for a while. The four doctors got after me and tried to convince me that it was best to have the licensed and supervised districts. I put it to them this way: If it is necessary here it is necessary at Kansas University and if I found that the best way, I must fight to have one established in every town in Kansas and a nice one at KU. That put a slightly different face on the question. I think that they were in earnest about the matter, but they were looking at it from a very narrow viewpoint."

Naismith was right that the people who favored prostitution would not give up. Within four days, he wrote home that two or three more houses were trying to start up, and the colonel had ordered him to meet with the civil authorities to get them shut down. "The mayor is a spineless sort of fellow and does not want to do anything that will hinder his political aspirations. Some of the regulars are acting as guardians for the colored women and unless we get the house cleaned out there may be trouble between the regulars and the militia. I am learning a whole lot about the meanness of some men and the goodness of others."

One lesson Naismith learned affected him personally. He was away from the camp on payday, when the transactions were handled in cash since the men were not near any banks. The adjutant who was supposed to keep Naismith's money for him spent it instead. When asked about it by Naismith, the soldier made up a story that the money had been stolen. When Naismith uncovered the truth, he did not demand his money. Other officers wanted him to press charges, but Naismith's attitude was that "he doesn't have the money, what's the use of worrying him about it?"

One of the secondary reasons Naismith wanted to keep the prostitution houses closed was so that the soldiers would not lose their money that way. He didn't want other soldiers to experience the same pain he felt when he had to go without money.

"You understand why I want to fight this battle against prostitution," he wrote in a letter home. "I am astonished that things have worked out so nicely and am afraid that it is the lull before the storm. Money is the root of this evil. Prostitution is bred and fostered by those who make money out of it.

"Several boys have lost their money already. A boy came in just a few minutes ago and told me his pocketbook had been taken. Men will sell their own souls, and the souls and bodies of others, for money. I would like to have a lot of it for you and the kiddies but not that way, never. Perhaps God does not want us to have too much for it might spoil the children."

In addition to trying to shut down the prostitution houses, Naismith began to give speeches to the Army soldiers, emphasizing how to prevent sexually transmitted diseases. In trying to develop alternative interests for the men, he once again turned to the sport of basketball.

He laid out an outdoor court, one he previously had used only in his physical education classes at Kansas. Two goals were set up, fifty feet apart. The biggest difference from the indoor game was that the court had an oval shape and the goals were farther inside the edges; thus, if a shot missed the goal, the ball would still likely be inbounds and in play rather than bouncing out of bounds and forcing the players to run to retrieve it—a useful system since there were no walls to stop it from rolling away.

Nine teams were formed among the troops at the Eagle Pass camp, and a tournament schedule was created. The sport did as Naismith had intended, creating another activity to keep the men occupied.

The soldiers also divided into baseball teams for frequent games, including one on a Sunday, which Naismith commented on in another letter home on August 13. "I am standing by the thing I have always said, that if there was no gate charged and the boys played for fun I had no objection to their playing on Sunday. You remember I suggested that when the legislature was wrestling with this matter . . . if there are any at home who object to Sunday baseball of this kind, say to them that it is a good healthy sport and better than lounging around. There is no money spent to make it anything but recreation. I am doing my best on the field and while I would like to have all the men read their Bibles, yet I want them to be good men and clean and strong."

While the Kansas militia and other National Guard units were patrolling the U.S.-Mexican border, Pershing's troops reluctantly gave up their search for Villa and returned to the Army bases. With the full-time soldiers now able to patrol the border, the National Guard units were allowed to return home.

On October 30, 1916, Naismith was discharged at Fort Riley and returned to Lawrence. His service to the military, however, was not over. The progress of World War I in Europe was making it more and more likely that the United States soon would be brought into that battle. It finally happened on April 6, 1917, when Congress passed a resolution declaring war against Germany.

It was not until several months later that the U.S. troops actually joined the fighting in France, however. General Pershing found most of the new recruits untrained, and he resisted the pressure of the British and French governments to send those soldiers to the front lines until they were more adequately prepared.

Naismith's work with the soldiers on the Mexican border had been noticed by the officials of the YMCA. One of the YMCA publications noted, "As an army chaplain on the Mexican border, Dr. Naismith fought practically single-handed the vice interests and the officials of the community near which his camp was located until he won. . . . He showed in this the same bulldog tenacity for which he was known when he played football against the big teams in the east in earlier days."

Naismith had been ordained as a minister so he could enlist in the National Guard and serve as a chaplain, but despite having lived and worked in the United States for 27 years, he still was not a U.S. citizen. That prevented him from joining the Army, something he wanted to do to show his support for the country that had given so much to him. Thus he went through the process of officially becoming a U.S. citizen, a task he completed in 1917.

Meanwhile, Army officials recognized the work that Naismith and the other chaplains had performed during the Mexican border conflict, and they knew similar work was going to be just as important to the welfare of the soldiers during the war in Europe. Officials of the National War Work Council asked Naismith to join their effort of instructing the U.S. soldiers, and he quickly agreed despite the advice of friends that, at age 56, he was entitled to stay home with his wife and children. His age didn't matter to Naismith. He felt he had been trained to work in this capacity, and that he simply was fulfilling his duty and obligation to his adopted country.

Naismith was appointed to the position in June 1917. He was one of a small group of lecturers whose job was to travel around the United States and conduct programs at the Army and Navy training camps to strengthen the moral character of the soldiers. He helped develop pamphlets, books, posters, cards, exhibits, slides, and films on sex education to use as part of his lectures.

His first tour took Naismith back to Texas, then on to Arizona and New Mexico. He wrote letters home as often as he could, describing his daily activities, and it was obvious to anyone how much he was enjoying the work. He believed he was making a difference in the lives of the young soldiers. "The more I see of the young men of the Army the more assured I am that they are like our own boys and girls, want to do what is right, but find it hard to do so when everyone else is doing the other thing," Naismith wrote in a letter dated June 20, 1917. "The government has done a great thing in making the cities clean up and giving the boys a chance to be good."

He was more discouraged when his tour made a stop in Douglass, Arizona, where he went to a police court and learned 50 women had been arrested the previous night. "Then I met some of the council of this place last night and got them started to clean up," he wrote. "This city is one of the worst Hell holes that I have ever seen for such a small place."

In a letter dated July 4, when he was in Albuquerque, New Mexico, Naismith wrote to his wife that "I do not know how much good I do down here but it is a great experience for me. I have talked to about 10,000 soldiers since leaving Lawrence and you ought to see them sit and listen. I know I am telling them things that they never thought about and am able to change their views on many subjects. In some crowds I have asked how many would fight this battle, against prostitution and venereal disease, as well as the other war, and every man present, almost, voted to keep himself clean and come home a Man. Oh it is great to see a bunch of these young fellows back up a proposition of this kind. . . .

"I talk to ministers—getting them down off their high horses and looking at things from a practical standpoint—then to businessmen, showing them where they are mistaken in their ideas—to judges and officials, correcting their mistakes from the biological and physiological standpoint. I feel I am fitted for this work."

One sergeant who came to one of Naismith's lectures said "he would like to have a moving picture of me as I got especially earnest. . . . He said it would make a great shadow-boxing film. I told one bunch of men who had been watching a boxing match that I felt good enough to try their champion in a bout . . . and you have no idea what an impression it made when I smacked my fist into my open hand and you could hear it a block away. It is a great advantage for me to know boxing and some of these other sports."

After a short visit home, Naismith left again for a tour of military camps in California, then returned to Texas. While he was home he got to see his first grandchild, a girl born to Margaret. He reflected on this trip home in a letter dated August 25, when he was back in San Antonio: "I did enjoy my trip home and one of the pleasantest memories is seeing you with little Peggy lying on your breast just as her mother did over twenty years ago. God made you a mother and you are a Grand mother, whether you will or no. And your mother spirit will go on down for generations. . . . Mother love is bigger than any other, for it is purely unselfish. . . . That stirs me up to do big things that I may be worthy of my partner."

The United States was now more than two months into the war in Europe, and additional troops—many of the same soldiers Naismith was counseling—were being shipped to the front lines every day. The YMCA and the National War Work Council were becoming increasingly concerned that services such as Naismith's were needed by the soldiers fighting the war in France. Dr. Exner, one of the Y leaders, asked Naismith about his interest in going to France and got a positive answer.

Exner wrote to Naismith, "We may have to call for you at any time, and if you go it will be as the prominent leader of that work there for the period of the war. It is our most strategic task, for if we do not handle the situation there, our accomplishments on this side will go to pieces over there."

On September 7, Naismith sent his wife a telegram that he would be home the following day. It was a quick visit and another goodbye. Four days later he was on a train for New York, and in less than two weeks he was on a transport ship en route to France, ready to do his part to help the United States emerge victorious in World War I.

• • •

CHAPTER 9

A Raging War

A trans-Atlantic journey in 1917 on a troop ship would not likely have been a very pleasurable experience under any circumstance, but with a world war raging, it was even more precarious. German submarines were patrolling the waters of the Atlantic Ocean, and German leaders had pledged to sink any transport ship carrying U.S. soldiers to the war in France. The YMCA workers were the same as soldiers to the Germans.

Naismith sent a letter to his wife from New York, before sailing for France. "We sail Sunday, probably, and it will take us about 13 days to cross, so you need not expect any letters from me for about four weeks after I start, but you will get them regularly after that until I get back. My mail will follow me and reach me a few days after I arrive in France. I will have a letter written so that if we meet a vessel we may exchange mail."

Before leaving, Naismith wrote again to his wife, "We are due to leave the dock but we may lay up somewhere for a day to throw any U-boats off track."

While Naismith may have had his personal doubts about the safety of the journey across the ocean, he had no doubts about the reasons he was being sent to France. Placed in charge of social hygiene for the American troops, he was told exactly what was expected of him. "It is a pretty big job," he said in a letter to his wife. "Go over and make the camps clean places for the boys to fight. And also get the right spirit into the men. That involves two things. Educate the men and eliminate the evils from the camps and vicinity. He [Dr. Exner] tells me that Pershing is very anxious to have this done and will probably help.

"I go without instructions to find out the best thing to do and then get the machinery working. . . . It is no child's play, especially when it is among the old-fashioned type of soldier and in France where ideals are so different. I am the only one doing this kind of work but as soon as it grows if we need men Dr. Exner will send over others to help me. The responsibility is great but I am going into it determined. I do wish that you and the family would pray for me, for I have never felt so much in need of help as I do at this present minute."

He added in another letter that he believed his trip was in keeping with his personal motto, "Leave the world a little better for my having lived in it."

As with any soldier going off to war, Naismith really had no idea how long he would be gone, and neither did his wife or children. Even with Margaret married, Maude was left to care for four children by herself, not an easy task, but the kind that a soldier's wife faces every time a war breaks out.

The ocean waters were rough, and Naismith reported to his wife that he had become seasick. "I was not what you would call sick but my meals did not taste good to me," he said. "I made a stagger at each one but my first breakfast consisted of a glass of water, as before the waiter could get my food I had disappeared to lie down in my berth.

"I am writing in the reading room. It is a beautiful place but I am afraid you would not enjoy it as there is a throb and a shiver that threatens my gastronomic equilibrium and even yet I beat a hasty retreat to my berth to let matters adjust themselves."

When he was not recovering from feeling sick, Naismith spent his time studying the French language, trying to learn as much as he could as quickly as possible. He told his wife, "When I lived in the college with a bunch of Frenchmen I could have learned the language without trying. I see so many things that I might have and should have done."

Naismith did arrive safely in Paris, but what he found there was not exactly a tourist's haven. At nights the lights were dimmed. The price of food was high, and certain foods were rationed or unavailable. Air raids were so common that most residents slept through them. Outside of Paris, in the rural countryside, living conditions were even worse.

He had been in Paris only four days when he experienced his first air raid warning, with the German bombers attacking the city. "I was awakened by the sound of hurrying feet in the halls . . . but we did not know what it meant," Naismith wrote. "We went out into the hall . . . and some of the older inhabitants were hurrying down [stairs] and some up. We found out those going down were seeking shelter while those going up were seeking adventure and the satisfying of their curiosity. It is easily imagined which way a tenderfoot would go. We secured a vantage point on the Hotel Gibraltar, from which we could see the lights of the airplanes and hear the whirring of the propellers."

More raids followed, and Naismith usually spent as much time noticing the reactions of the French citizens as he did making certain he was not in the line of fire or of any falling shrapnel. "It was interesting to watch the psychology of the people," he wrote. "You would hear a bomb drop only a short distance away and you knew that in all probability there were some killed and perhaps many wounded, but the only feeling was one of curiosity. I tried to analyze the attitude of mind in which there was no fear shown for in all the time I saw only a very few who were really afraid. It seemed that the people had reckoned there were only about 10 chances in 1 million of being injured, and they were willing to take that chance."

Naismith's headquarters were in Paris, but for the 19 months he was in France, he was there usually only between assignments. He spent much of his time in the military camps, near the front lines, talking and working directly with the soldiers. Particularly on the front lines, the soldiers faced terrible hygiene and sanitary conditions, often going weeks without a shower or bath. When temperatures were not below freezing, the soldiers lived in trenches filled with mud. Disease was rampant, and many soldiers contracted typhoid. Naismith experienced some of the same rough conditions as the soldiers—the mud and filth and the long, cold nights. He also had the responsibility of trying to rise above the horrible conditions because he was there to brighten the spirits of the troops.

In his letters home, he often did not mention the intolerable conditions, both because he did not want his family to worry and because his letters were usually subject to the control of a censor. For that reason he was not allowed to say where he was writing from, and he was reluctant to tell his wife and family how much he loved them. "I cannot tell you about our work here; I cannot give information even to Dr. Exner," he said. "That hinders cooperation, but military laws must be obeyed. I am so busy that I have no time to be lonesome but you need not think that you are forgotten for you are my inspiration and good genius."

Naismith faced other challenges as well, including the language barrier. "I had quite an experience with a hotel keeper the other day," he wrote in a letter dated October 12, 1917. "I wanted two rooms for myself and Demarest and I could make her understand all right for myself but I could not think what the word for friend was, and when I said my friend she said 'oui, oui' and pointed to herself. At last I told her that my brother wanted a room and that produced the desired result. I will have more sympathy for a stranger in a strange land after this. . . . The natives talk so fast and run their words together so that I cannot make them out and when I do not understand they hurry things up a little. I know now exactly how you feel when I am talking and you cannot hear."

In a letter a month later to Fred Wills, a friend from Vinland, Kansas, Naismith again described the difficulties he was having with the French language. "The thing that I miss most here is the touch of the children," he wrote. "I cannot talk French well enough to speak to any of the little ones here and I have not met a child that spoke American since leaving New York. Tell the children that I often think of them sitting up in the choir seats or on the front rows and can see their faces looking at me. . . . Tell them how thankful they ought to be that they live in America, and every time I see a child running around in wooden shoes I think they cannot have much fun with that kind of athletic footwear. On the cobblestones you can hear them a block away when they run. All the boys from five to thirteen wear short pants and low stockings and their bare knees give me the shivers. . . . But they seem to act very much like our children."

Naismith settled into a routine of lecturing and talking to the soldiers, organizing groups of soldiers to help out others when he was not there, and sending out literature and other publications he thought would be helpful to the soldiers. As had been the case during his service along the Mexican border, he was interested primarily in closing down prostitution houses, or at least keeping the American soldiers from going there. He also tried to use athletics again as a diversion, and that tactic frequently worked. Boxing matches especially proved to be a popular form of entertainment.

"Two weeks ago I went to a port city when the troops were coming in," Naismith wrote. "The first night there was a big boxing tournament and between bouts I got into the ring and talked to the boys for about 20 minutes, putting up manliness to them. . . . Afterwards I was watching the boxing when a sailor who had a shot or two under his belt became quarrelsome and they could not get him home to his ship. I stepped over and shook hands

with him and began to talk to him, jollying him along and pull-
ing on his hand. . . . I got him out of the building and started for
his ship. Then he ran back to talk some more and I had to go a
little farther with him and bade him good night; then his chums
began to thank me and he did the same, and I had to walk a little
further with him. The last I saw of him he was walking off to his
ship talking over his shoulder to me."

Naismith later reflected that even though he never held a pastorate, the closest he came to preaching was during his two years
in France—in an indirect way. Too many of the soldiers were
going into a French village near their base and getting themselves
in trouble. Naismith and his coworkers decided to set up a boxing ring near the camp entrance. "We would start a lively match
about the time the boys began starting 'on leave.'" Naismith said.
"They stopped to watch, then begged to participate, and the next
thing they knew it was time to be back in quarters. Prize fights
may sound like strange preaching, but they did the work."

Naismith was doing his work at the cost of his own physical
health. He admitted in a letter home, dated January 16, 1918,
about four months after his arrival in France, that he had lost 28
pounds. He insisted, though, that he felt "fit as a fiddle and in fine
fighting fettle," no doubt to try to keep his wife and children from
worrying about him and the conditions he was experiencing.

One of those conditions was extreme cold, which was why he
was glad to receive a new pair of woolen socks knitted for him by
his daughters. "We all knitted things for him and sent him pack-
ages as often as possible," Hellen Naismith wrote. "After receiving one pair of socks knitted for him he wrote back and wanted
to know which foot was the longest, as one sock was fully an inch
and a half longer than the other."

Receiving that package no doubt produced a smile on Naismith's face, and he also was happy to see his former boss at
the YMCA Training School, Dr. Gulick, and his wife when they
arrived in Paris for a visit and to check on the YMCA workers.
Another encouragement came from a Long Island man, who sent

a package of tobacco and candy to distribute to a group of soldiers. "I took it back to camp and set it at a table giving them their choice of tobacco or candy, and the candy ran our first," Naismith wrote.

There were no doubts in Naismith's mind, or in the minds of anyone who read his letters home, that he was in the middle of a war. He saw the results first hand when a munitions factory in Paris exploded. He talked about the aftermath in a letter to Maude dated February 15, 1918:

"I spent all the afternoon helping in the hospital taking care of the wounded. Mr. Johnson and I were sitting at dinner about five miles from the explosion and the doors of the restaurant were blown open. . . . Some of the windows along the street were broken. We thought it was a daylight raid. A great cloud arose off to the south.

"McCurdy, Dr. Lord and I started out in a car to see if we could help but the wounded that could be found were carried into hospitals so we went over to one and set to work dressing wounds. They were mostly scalp wounds and cuts from broken glass and falling timbers. We worked until 6 P.M. before we finished. The part of the city near the factory was pretty well shattered, windows smashed in and roofs blown off. I do not believe that any of those in the mill could possibly escape. The terrific shock was enough to throw them in every direction."

By March 1918, the Germans had begun a more intense attack on Paris. Guns were firing bombs at the city from an unheard-of distance of 75 miles, making it almost impossible to mount a defense. The guns, nicknamed Big Bertha, were the Germans' last hopes to capture Paris and win the war.

Naismith knew that his wife and children would be worried about him, so in another letter he tried to reassure them about his safety, despite the war raging around him:

"I suppose that you will read almost as I am writing that we are being bombarded, big shells dropping into Paris every 20 minutes," he wrote. "They make a terrific explosion and scatter things around quite a bit but there is no sign of panic. I have no idea where these come from, the papers say from 75 miles away but this seems an impossibility. . . . I cannot see any good of bombarding Paris while the big drive is on.

"Now Nell [his nickname for Hellen], don't let your mother worry about me for we are just about as safe as you are there at home regardless of the little extra momentary trouble. We are in no sense foolhardy. I feel perfectly safe because I know that the right will succeed, and that we are all in good hands."

Maude, of course, continued to worry about her husband and sent a cable to Paris to make certain he was still alive. Naismith returned the cable with the answer that yes, he was alive, and followed it with another letter: "I have made arrangements that if anything should happen, which is very unlikely, they would cable you at once. Don't you worry. There is no more danger here than at home. I often think that there is more danger walking along the streets of being run over by a taxi than there is of being hurt by a bomb or a shell."

Three days after that letter was written, on March 26, Naismith was reminded that the violence and danger were very real despite the reassurances he was giving to his wife. The Germans continued to bomb Paris with regularity. An attack on the church of St. Gervais on Good Friday was particularly deadly, leaving 156 people killed or wounded.

Two days later, Naismith admitted in another letter that the war seemed to be getting closer to a resolution, one way or the other. "The war is a horrible thing," he wrote, "but it seems now as if something decisive would happen soon. I have said all the year that Germany had to do one of three things to satisfy her people: beat the British by taking Calais; beat the French by taking Paris; or stop America from coming across the ocean. If she cannot do any one of these she is beaten in the eyes of her own people. She is making a big effort to do any of them and is failing. . . . She will have neither the money, the means, nor the men to make another big effort. I believe that good will prevail."

Through April and May, the Germans' advance toward Paris continued as they took control of villages and towns en route. The troops got as close as 37 miles from Paris, where the resistance stiffened. By mid-July, the Allied forces had forced the Germans back across the Marne River.

Naismith continued his work behind the front lines and in the port cities, working with the soldiers on an individual basis and also offering his lectures and talks about sex education and the evils of prostitution. "The human heart in a black or white skin wants to see right prevail," he wrote in a letter to Maude. "I tell them pretty plain truths and make them feel mean for their own errors, yet they recognize the truth of it. My duty is to sow the seed of truth and God will send the influences to make it grow. I sometimes get pretty blue for my subject is not one that appeals to men, but when I present it faithfully I seldom fail to get a hearty response."

The moments that seemed to energize Naismith the most came when he happened to run into a soldier who had been a student at Kansas. Several former students were members of Company M, which also had been deployed on the Mexican border when Naismith was assigned to that region. He often considered the company to be superior, especially physically, to other units in the Army. He once hiked 15 miles in the middle of the winter to deliver a heavy duffel bag full of newspapers and letters from home to the Kansas soldiers.

Whenever Naismith heard there were some Kansans in a camp, he made a special effort to meet with them. Usually, when the soldiers heard he was there, they would go out of their way to come up to him. He saw the sons of other university professors, and he wrote home and told Maude to assure their parents that they were in good shape and doing well.

Naismith realized that most of the letters he wrote home were subject to the review of a censor before they could be mailed, and he joked about that in a letter to Maude on May 30: "I have tried to observe the censorship rules, but it does seem so odd to have your letter read by a third party. If the censor does not know how to write a fine letter it will not be for want of having plenty of examples."

Two weeks later, on Mother's Day, Naismith used the occasion to profess his love and admiration for his wife once again, regardless of whether the censor was going to be reading the letter. Naismith didn't need a special occasion to share his feelings with his wife, but he no doubt had been pleased when President Wilson officially proclaimed the second Sunday in May as Mother's Day in 1914, hoping it would inspire more tributes to women throughout the country.

Naismith's letter said it came from "somewhere in France," and it was addressed to "My own dear 'Mother of Mine.'"

"(And you certainly are the mother of those five children of mine—therefore the 'mother of mine')," Naismith wrote. "This is Mother's Day and I want to tell you how much I appreciate your motherly (as well as wifely) care for me, for you have taken the place of a mother to me on many occasions, and have made up to me the loss of my own mother. . . . Your gentleness and love have made the years in which I have known you so full and blessed that it seems as if they could not have held any more happiness. . . . Your mother instinct is so great . . . a true, faithful, intelligent, wise and loving mother for our children. . . . Accept, my dear, this imperfect expression of a perfect admiration and love. . . . It is not only on Mother's Day, it is every day. . . . And it grows with each return of the morning sun. . . . Dear heart, I hope that you will read between the lines a love that is pure as the color of the paper between the strokes of this halting pen."

Even though Naismith had predicted that the end of the war was drawing close, it was in fact many months away. He did not let himself get discouraged, however, and tried to find simple pleasures wherever he could. "I was out at a camp this forenoon and held services in the mess hall of the barracks," he wrote on June 30. "There was no one to lead the singing, so I had to do that. Imagine how hard that was, for my music has not improved any but over here we never hesitate to do what is necessary. I had a nice time chatting with the boys."

The attacks on Paris from Big Berthas continued, with the eventual total of many hundreds of people killed or wounded, a million people driven out of the city, and millions of dollars in property damage, but still the Germans could not infiltrate and capture the city. The Allied forces held, and eventually forced the Germans to retreat.

In addition to facing the daily challenges of the war, Naismith and other Allied forces found themselves battling another enemy. An influenza pandemic, which had spread throughout the United States, was also leaving soldiers sick in France and across Europe. Nearly 40 percent of the American troops who arrived in France came through the port city of Brest, and it was from there that the disease spread. As the soldiers were dispatched throughout France, they carried the influenza strain with them, affecting not only the soldiers from the United States and other countries but also the civilians of France.

In John Barry's *The Great Influenza*, he reports that "in October, at the peak of the epidemic in Paris, 4,574 people had died there of influenza or pneumonia. The disease had never entirely left that city." The deaths continued for months, and it was quite likely that Naismith lost more soldiers to the pandemic than he saw killed by battles with the Germans. Throughout the world, more people did die from the pandemic than were killed in the war. Ironically, there is substantial evidence that the beginning of the flu epidemic was in Kansas, according to Barry.

Naismith knew the war would eventually end, and he had some opportunities to think about the future and whether he wanted to return to the University of Kansas. He asked Maude what she thought, and she responded in a letter dated July 8, 1918. "I want you to do just exactly as you want to do," she wrote. "I imagine the work here would seem very narrow after what you have been doing. I am working to clear up our responsibilities here so if anything comes you will be free to do as you think best.

The University of Kansas has not progressed in the last few years, rather it has gone the other way. They have never given us a cent of the money they owe us. Your gymnasium is turned into living quarters for the men in training; the beautiful grass is tramped brown, men by the dozens lying around everywhere, they have not received their uniforms yet and they wear overalls and one-piece suits and I can tell you the sight is anything but picturesque. They are not college men, mostly mechanics. Honnie [Hellen] said she was glad she saw them before they received their uniforms. Perhaps it won't be so very long before our boys will be marching or rather sailing home again."

Naismith responded that he had not made up his mind about his future plans. He was on an official leave of absence until the end of the war, and he said he had received a letter from the chancellor, but the letter "did not say anything about my coming back."

In addition to wondering about his own plans, Naismith was thinking about all of the military men who would be coming home when the war was over. "We have a big work ahead of us to prepare the country for the homecoming of the boys," Naismith wrote. "Many are coming home bigger and better men. But the folks at home must prepare the social conditions so that America will be a better place in which to bring up the next generation."

Summer turned into fall, and the war lingered. Maude gave up any hope that her husband would return soon. She fell seriously ill in October, but just as Naismith never let her know how he was doing physically, she said nothing to him, nor did their children, until she had recovered. By that time, he had decided to return to Kansas, "if they will give me the right kind of work to do."

"There are a great deal of data there that would be valuable for working up statistics," Naismith wrote to Maude. "I hope they have not disturbed my files too seriously for I have been keeping information for a good many years for this very fact, that I might have data for statistical work. But I am not going to worry about any of those things."

It was just as well that Naismith did not spend time worrying about it, because when he did return to Kansas he learned to his dismay that the Army officers who occupied his office had thrown away all of his files.

One more immediate worry came in early October, when he had to leave Paris to visit a camp. "We left at 4 P.M., drove 50 miles to a camp, had a splendid meeting, then drove 50 miles back," he explained. "On the way our lights went out and we had quite a time driving in the dark, especially when we came to a woods. Then we had a puncture and we got out and fixed that. Got home OK at 2 A.M. and had a splendid sleep with my cold feet in my sheepskin slippers."

That was only a momentary diversion from what Naismith spent most of his time that fall thinking about, which was how the United States was going to treat its soldiers when they returned home from the war. On October 13, he wrote, "This morning's papers tell us that Germany has accepted all terms, and I know that this will bring cheer to many hearts, but this does not mean that everything is settled or that we can get home immediately, for it may be months. Indeed in some ways our work is just the most needed.

"I hope America will prepare to take care of the boys in the right way. The trouble is that she will make a great fuss over them for a couple of weeks, then forget all about them. I have a plan to give the boys a chance to make good themselves when they return, without any idea of charity or dependence. I am going to send it to [Kansas] Governor Capper and he can do as he pleases about it. How I wish I could talk it over with you and get your opinion; it is too long to wait to get your answer, but maybe you can push it from the home end."

Before he had a chance to write and tell Maude more about his plan, Naismith had another letter to write—the celebration had begun in Paris; the war was over. On November 12, 1918, Naismith wrote to his son Jack: "The 'DAY' has arrived but not the one that the Kaiser planned when he talked about 'der Tag' nor is the celebration that is going on outside the kind that pleases him. He is no better sport than he has been all along when he loses, he is not man enough to come out and say, 'I have lost,' but he asks refuge of the Netherlands, the nation that he badgered and bullied almost beyond endurance. We can hardly yet conceive of the kind of nature that would act as he has done. It looks like another symptom of paranoia.

"Well, the war is over, and now we can get down to the business of making the world a decent place to live in. I do not know how much longer I should stay here. It will be June or July at least. I know that Mamma will be disappointed if I do not get back right away but I hope that if I cannot return immediately conditions will be such that she can come over here. Surely she has earned a trip abroad."

A day later, Naismith had time to write to his wife and give her more information about his plan to help the soldiers returning home from the war. Amazingly, what Naismith outlined was almost a draft of the GI Bill, officially known as the Servicemen's Readjustment Act, which was passed by Congress near the end of the Second World War, in 1944, almost 26 years after Naismith came up with his idea.

The bill passed by Congress and signed into law by President Franklin Roosevelt called for servicemen to receive college or vocational training, one year of unemployment compensation, and the opportunity to get loans to buy houses or start a business. How did that compare to Naismith's plan? He described his idea in the letter to Maude:

My plan for the returning soldiers is this . . . I want the young men to settle down and to buy a home. You and I kept putting it off . . . and we would have been a good deal further ahead if we had started sooner. I want to make it possible for everyone of the boys to start in on that purchase right away. Take Lawrence for instance—say one of the boys who was engaged or who married just before leaving wants to settle down there in the dry goods business. See that he gets a job of some kind—no more pay than any other man who is doing the same work and certainly no less. Let him select the part of town in which he would like to live. Let the city or an organization buy a couple of lots for him and give him the deed—with restrictions on its resale, of course. He could then have the Building and Loan Association put up a home for him and he would pay it off as he could. In certain cases he could be relieved from making any payments for two or three years so he could furnish his home. Or if there was a house already erected that he would like, make it possible for him to purchase that, on terms that would let him go ahead. The idea is to make it possible for him to start a home right away.

The hard part for a young man is to get the first start, especially if it costs as much to buy flowers, candy, etc., for your girl as it would cost to make up the difference between the care of one and of two. The first couple of years of marriage are the critical ones. . . . It would be good for the young man, and doubly good for the young wife, as she has something to work for.

It is also worthwhile from the economic side as every home is an asset to a community and would be worth the time and money spent, if looked at purely from a money point of view.

I feel that this would be the logical outcome of our attempt over here to keep the boys fit for a home. The community should adapt itself to the nature of boys and girls as much as possible. I believe the solution of the problems will lie more in making preparations for it right now, than in a multitude of lectures afterward. If these boys settle down it will help all our growing boys to settle down.

This is weighing on my heart and I would like to see it pushed at home.

It was obvious how much attention Naismith was devoting to the topic when it became the subject of another letter to Maude, dated 10 days later, on November 23:

When the boys return home they will be about two years behind the ones who stayed there and made money. It is only fair then that this disadvantage should be overcome. Many of them would have been married by this time and would have started a home. All of them, while over here, have gotten a big idea of home and are anxious to settle down.

I want to see it made possible for the young married men to get a start with a home. For the engaged men, whose sweethearts have been waiting for them, to get married right away. And for some others who have made up their minds to settle down, to prepare a home for the one whom they shall choose. . . . Many of the boys have been looking forward to settling down and if they do they will make good citizens.

But if they have to drag along they will postpone the time when they will assume responsibility and will again get the wandering foot and become irresponsible. Or if too much hero worship is given they will not be content to settle down.

This is a critical period in the moral, domestic and social life of the returning soldier. . . . But it seems that my work is here so I will try to get someone else to do it at home.

Despite his best efforts and intentions, Naismith was unable to see his dream plan become reality. Whether it would have been different had he returned to the United States immediately after the end of the war instead of remaining in France for several additional months will never be known. It is obvious that he never found a supporter with enough political clout to push his plan through legislative channels.

One person who might have been able to help was Naismith's old boss, Dr. Gulick, but shortly after Gulick had visited France, he had returned home and died. He was only 53 years old. Friends later said that Gulick knew he had only a few months to live when he came to France, but wanted to make the trip anyway.

It can be speculated that if Naismith's precursor to the GI Bill had been passed and implemented by Congress, many of the financial problems suffered by World War I veterans during the Great Depression could have been lessened or avoided altogether. Instead, with no support from the government, thousands of veterans lost their jobs and homes during the Depression and eventually organized a march on Washington in 1932. As many as 25,000 soldiers and their families set up camp in tents along the Anacostia River, demanding immediate help from the government. When it didn't come, they marched up and down Pennsylvania Avenue for three days before President Hoover ordered active soldiers, led by General Douglas MacArthur, to disperse the crowds and dismantle the camp.

Gulick's death and Naismith's disappointment at the failure of his plan for veterans did not lessen his enthusiasm about the success of his work in France. On Thanksgiving Day in 1918, Naismith wrote a long letter to his wife detailing the 10 things he was most thankful for in his life. Listed seventh was "the knowledge that I have tried to help the people of the world to make it a little better, and that I have tried to love my neighbor as myself. That there is no great thing in my past life that makes me steep my soul in remorse. Thanks to God and my mother's memory in my youth, and to the helpmate of my life in maturity years."

By this time, Naismith was witnessing a return of the beauty of the city of Paris. For months he tried to convince his wife to make a trip across the Atlantic to join him. "I have not had a word from you written since the Armistice," he wrote on December 6. "I suppose you had a jubilation over there. We certainly had a time here. I stood on top of a big cannon to watch the procession go by and had a fine view. Paris is a very different place now from what it was when the lights were all out. Now everything is gay and getting back to its old-time swing."

As he came closer to completing his work for the YMCA, Naismith made one last request to his wife to join him, and he also began to make plans to return to Kansas. "I wish you would come over," he said in a letter on February 22. "The only other thing is to come to Scotland and then come over from there. . . . I had a letter from Dean Lemplin asking me if I was planning to return to the University of Kansas. I have written him, and will enclose a copy of the letter so you will know what I have suggested. I want a budget big enough so that I can work efficiently, and can keep in touch with what is going on in other parts of the country. I do like Kansas as a state though it is not much on climate, especially in the summer. This country is damp and foggy and it rains nearly every day when it does not snow or freeze."

Packing up his office to begin his journey home, Naismith reminisced about the 19 months he had spent in France. "Some of my German souvenirs that I picked up on the battlefields have been stolen out of my office," he wrote. "They were not valuable but they were picked up by myself—especially a German helmet that I found in a trench just south of Soissons, where the Marines did such good work. . . . I have one souvenir that I think a lot of. It is a basketball used by the British in a game on the battlefield of Lille, in one of the first games they played. The British army is making basketball one of its games."

He also returned home with a copy of a book that included a French translation of the original basketball rules, published in 1897, and with the memory of having seen basketball hoops near the front lines of the Battle of Belleau Wood, evidence that his game had been played by soldiers within range of the German guns. He also brought home a small fragment of a shell the Germans had fired during the bombardment of Paris.

As he left France, Naismith received a letter from one of his YMCA co-workers, Dr F. N. Seerley:

> I want to express to you in writing what I have reminded you of several times in personal conversations, namely my high regard for your personality, for your absolute devotion to the cause, for your human interest in the boys whom you came to interest and change, for your deep personal touch and friendship which has not only meant so much to me but to every one who has come into fellowship with you even to a slight degree, for your patience and cooperation in every effort that we have made in the direction of achieving our hope. Had we not had such a confidence in you, we could not have devoted ourselves so absolutely to our task. Had we not had so much confidence in your leadership, we could not have accepted your suggestions with so much sincerity and willingness.
>
> History will show by and by what you have done and we, who have been associated with you, will have a part in writing that history.

Sailing on board the *Rochambeau* ocean liner, Naismith took time to thank Seerley for his letter. In a return letter he said, "As I look back over my time spent in France, it seems as if we had been able only to nibble at the corners in our work, but when I think of the number of men to whom we have spoken there must be quite a few who have been helped, probably some whom we never would have reached in any other way. After all what we have to do is sow the seed and the Master provides the sunshine and the rain to make it grow."

A telegram gave Maude Naismith the news that her husband was en route home, and two weeks after leaving Paris, he stepped off the train in Kansas City where his family was waiting. They barely recognized him.

"When my father left the United States, he weighed 200 pounds," Hellen Naismith recalled. "When he stepped off the train in Kansas City, he only weighed 145 pounds. The climate in France did not agree with him and he had bronchitis all the time he was there. My youngest brother [Jim] who was only four when he left, had to become acquainted with him all over again."

That was only one of the tasks awaiting Naismith on his return home.

CHAPTER 10

Happy Homecoming

Naismith was happy to be reunited with his family and to be away from the horrors of the war. He gradually built his weight back to his accustomed 185 pounds, and he resumed his work teaching the various physical education classes at the university.

He also returned to his teaching at the Presbyterian church on Sunday. During the war, he had relaxed his feelings about how people should act on the Sabbath, and now he decided one Sunday to combine a baseball scoreboard with a game of Bible stories. When a question was missed, it was considered a strike. As in baseball, three strikes meant you were out. The church elders got so upset with Naismith for what they considered an act of hedonism that they removed him from his position teaching the class.

When word spread to nearby churches, the popular Naismith found himself in great demand as a speaker, and this created another opportunity for him, which lasted almost the rest of his life. He became a visiting minister, traveling to churches not only in Lawrence but as far as 60 miles away to fill in when the church's regular minister was away. For smaller churches that could not afford a full-time preacher, Naismith became a regular guest, receiving either $5 or $10 to preach on Sunday morning and to cover his expenses.

Naismith went to Vinland, Kansas, on alternate Sundays, and later preached at churches in Rossville and Delia. Since his salary from the university was only $200 a month, the extra income was a great boost for the family. In May 1923 he wrote himself a note to remember to save the money from the Rossville and Delia churches to pay the family's living expenses in August and September.

Naismith traveled to the neighboring towns by train or by his surrey if the weather cooperated. It was not until the early 1920s that the Naismith family finally got its first car, a used Studebaker, and Naismith was reluctant to learn how to drive. His son Jack became his regular chauffeur, until Naismith finally realized he was going to have to learn how to drive himself.

By this time the family car was a Model T Ford, and Naismith was not a good driver. He drove as if he were still working with a team of horses, and he forgot that he had to put his foot on the brake to stop the car. He thought it should stop when he stood up, pulled up on the steering wheel, and yelled "whoa, whoa." That was what worked with the horses. His sons Jack and Jim got so tired of repairing holes in the garage wall that they built an iron rail in the back of the garage to prevent their father from driving through the wall.

Naismith regularly drove his car into a ditch, however, and one time, in Kansas City, he ran a stop sign and was pulled over by a police officer. "Didn't you see that boulevard stop?" the officer asked. Naismith reportedly responded, "What's a boulevard stop?" The police officer gave up and let him go.

On a trip to his native Canada, to visit his sister Annie and Uncle Peter, the family was camping by the side of the road. Their tent was designed so that one side attached to the car and the other side could be pegged to the ground. When Maude was preparing supper and found she needed bread, Naismith quickly volunteered to get some. He hopped into the driver's seat, and before anybody could stop him, he pulled away, bringing the tent flapping next to him.

In the summer of 1922 Naismith found a secondary job other than preaching. Jack Naismith and two of his friends had decided to work as laborers on a road gang near Chapman, Kansas. As Naismith was telling his son and friends goodbye, he remarked, "I wish I could go with you." One of Jack's friends told him to come along, so he did.

Naismith got a job driving a team of horses, and none of the other workers had any idea about his true identity. He, his son, and friends enjoyed a good laugh when the work ended and he resumed his "regular" job at the university.

One of the reasons Naismith was such an effective preacher was the same as the reason for his popularity and success as a teacher. He was able to talk to people on their own level, speaking a language that they understood. He also was not afraid to make himself the subject of a joke, nor was he afraid to challenge his students and get into a healthy discussion of any particular issue.

Unfortunately for Naismith, as he settled back into his teaching and administrative role at the university, there seemed to be one man who was always getting in his way—his former student and player, Forrest "Phog" Allen.

Allen had been away from Lawrence longer than Naismith, leaving in 1909 to begin his osteopathy training, and then coaching in Warrensburg, Missouri, at what is now Central Missouri State University. W. O. Hamilton had succeeded Allen as Kansas's basketball coach in 1909, but Hamilton resigned after the 1918–1919 season to devote more time to his Chevrolet car dealership.

Track coach Karl Schlademan was chosen to take over the basketball team as well, but the university also wanted to hire a manager of athletics. The choice came down to either Allen or Bert Kennedy, who had coached football at Kansas from 1904 to 1910. Kennedy wanted the job and was endorsed by Naismith, and he appeared to be the choice of most alumni. One person who was against him, however, had an important voice—the chancellor, Frank Strong.

Strong would cast a vote only if the school's 10-member athletic board deadlocked on a choice, but he let it be known that he preferred Allen. The five students and five faculty members did not need Strong's vote, reaching a 7–2 decision in favor of Allen, and he was hired.

After one game, Schlademan resigned as the basketball coach, saying he had decided to concentrate on his duties with the track team. With no time to find another coach, Allen—who was also coaching the freshman team—appointed himself as the basketball coach, a job he would retain until 1956.

Naismith was still the director of the physical education department in 1920, but that was now viewed as a separate job from the manager of athletics. Naismith had no official role with any of the Kansas intercollegiate teams.

Naismith and Allen never openly clashed, but they also had little to do with each other. Their offices were on separate floors in Robinson Gymnasium, and Naismith never dropped in when the men's basketball team was practicing. It was obvious that Naismith and Allen had different approaches to their jobs, and a difference in attitude about their work. Allen's most publicized slogan was that he taught his teams to "play to win," while Naismith always maintained that he wanted his athletes to do their best, but it didn't really matter to him whether they won or not. Naismith said often that sports should fulfill three purposes: to play for the fun of playing, to engage in physical activity to aid the overall development of the body, and to learn sportsmanship through being a member of a team. Winning was never mentioned as a goal by Naismith.

In his autobiography, posthumously published in 1941, Naismith wrote that the lessons he sought to teach through sports were to "let us all be able to lose gracefully and to win courteously, to accept criticism as well as praise, and last of all, to appreciate the attitude of the other fellow at all times."

Though Allen almost appeared jealous of Naismith's popularity with his students, he often told Naismith he could not understand why he spent so much time working with students. Even when Naismith was not teaching, he was frequently meeting with and counseling students about both academic and personal matters. Students often came to his house during the evening. Even though he had little money, he frequently loaned what he had to students who, he said, needed it more than he did. Naismith never kept a record of the transaction or worried about whether the student would pay him back.

One incident illustrated the division between Allen and Naismith. When Allen saw one of his basketball players coming out from a meeting in Naismith's office, Allen asked Naismith about the nature of the meeting, to which Naismith reportedly replied, "If he wanted you to know, he would have told you."

Many times Naismith would be too busy to go to class, so he often would ask his son-in-law, George Stanley, then working as a student instructor, to substitute for him. The popular saying around the Kansas campus was that Naismith was "never too busy to help a boy."

Unofficially he served as a dean of men, and he was often the first person students thought of calling when there was trouble. When one of two students swimming in Potter Lake in the middle of the night went under the water and drowned, Naismith was one of the first people called to come to the scene, and it was he who notified the boy's parents.

The conflict between Allen and Naismith basically consisted of a difference of opinion about the value and importance of athletics. It was ultimately a question of whether intercollegiate athletics should exist to make money for the university—making the athletes essentially professional in nature—or should exist primarily for the development of the college students themselves.

Naismith had strong opinions on the issue, dating as far back as 1911, when he gave his speech on commercialism in sports. He also showed his opinion by working to develop and promote intramural games for all university students.

One disagreement between the two men concerned selling tickets to the men's basketball games. By 1920, the games had been moved to the new Hoch Auditorium, where general admission tickets sold for 35 cents and reserved seats cost 50 cents. Allen wanted to use the strong interest in basketball that was developing on campus to generate as many sold tickets as possible, while Naismith considered selling tickets an exploitation of the student athletes. Allen argued that bringing money in to the university through the sale of basketball tickets would benefit the other university sports as well.

Frank Strong had been replaced as the Kansas chancellor in 1920 by Ernest Lindley, and to Naismith's disappointment, Lindley agreed with Allen. Lindley made numerous changes in administrative personnel at the university in his first few years on the job, and ultimately, in 1924, he made the decision to replace Naismith as the chairman of the Department of Physical Education. Lindley appointed Allen to serve in that position along with his other roles.

Students and colleagues who knew both Allen and Naismith stress that the disagreements between the two men were always about philosophy and never became personal. In fact, Allen was Naismith's guest on fishing trips to Canada over the next several years.

Allen, on multiple occasions, tried to ensure that Naismith's role in history as the inventor of basketball was never forgotten. One such example came in 1920, when Allen discovered there was no photo or mention of Naismith in the basketball rule book for that season. After Allen protested to the publisher, Naismith's name and photo were included in the book.

When Naismith was in Lawrence, he attended the men's games, but observers said they never saw him stand up or cheer, applaud, or give any sign of emotion whatsoever. Part of the reason, no doubt, was that Naismith objected to many of the rules changes that were coming to basketball. "Don't get too far away from the original game," he once cautioned. "It was the best game."

Allen already was establishing his legacy, and by 1923 he had a talented group of players on his team. Led by Paul Endacott, the program's first Hall of Fame player, the Kansas Jayhawks went 16–0 in the Missouri Valley Conference, the first undefeated record in the conference's history, and the team was unofficially recognized as the national champion. Another member of that team was Adolph Rupp, who went on to become a legendary coach at the University of Kentucky.

Naismith's only true involvement with that team was when Allen insisted that he be included in the official team picture, which features the two coaches surrounded by the 11 players.

Naismith was 62 years old when he was forced out as chairman of the Department of Physical Education in 1924, but in no way was he ready to retire. He had lost his positions as the chapel director, basketball coach, university physician, and now as the chairman of his department. Still, he was energetic, active, in good physical shape, and determined to maintain his role of teaching at the university as long as possible. No doubt upset by the chancellor's decision, he never spoke about the issue or showed any visible signs of distress. Instead, he threw himself even harder into his teaching assignments, devoting more of his time to meeting with and counseling students on an individual basis.

Naismith also became a popular speaker around the country, using the forum to offer his opinions about basketball, athletics in general, and, of course, religion. Often, he would arrive in town unannounced and would not be recognized until it was time for him to speak. Once he was an invited guest at the Indiana state high school championship game in Indianapolis, but guards would not let him in the gym because they said it was too crowded. The police were called, and when Naismith explained the problem, he was asked to identify himself. Hearing his name, the officer said, "Good Lord, man, why didn't you say so long ago?"

Naismith also went to Iowa once to visit his son and to deliver a speech at Morningside College. Before the speech, he saw a pickup game going on in the gym, and one player asked Naismith if he would be their referee. Another player spoke up, "That old duffer never saw a game of basketball." The boy apologized that night at the banquet.

His students at Kansas, however, never showed Naismith any disrespect. They were always assured that Naismith would keep his class interesting and that he valued their opinions when a discussion arose.

"He taught all of his classes with almost boundless enthusiasm," Dr. Ed Elbel, a physical education professor at Kansas from 1928 to 1937 and a close friend of Naismith, told the *University Daily Kansan* in a 1973 interview. "He challenged his students with questions, which often resulted in heated arguments. When he emerged from the classroom with his necktie askew and part of his shirttail hanging over his belt, his colleagues knew that 'Doc' had had a good class session."

In a paper presented at a conference in Portland, Oregon, in 1970, Henry Shenk, a student at Kansas from 1924 to 1928, offered many anecdotes about Naismith's work in the classroom. One of his Naismith's duties, Shenk recalled, "was to teach a required class of hygiene once a week to freshmen men":

On this particular occasion in the spring of 1925, the class was being held in a second floor classroom in old Robinson Gym. The day was warm and the 60 freshmen crowded into the room were being given a lesson on venereal disease. The room was even warmer because the shades over the windows, which were the only source of ventilation, had to be drawn to darken the room to show a series of slides. These slides had been developed by the Army for use in their social hygiene program in World War I. The slides were horrible, showing the most advanced cases of syphilis and designed, no doubt, to scare the recruits of 1917 so badly that they would take no chances.

As the lecture went on, the air became hotter and muggier. Suddenly there was a thump. A boy had fainted. Naismith called out, "let him lay" and went ahead with the lecture. Then there was another thump. Another had fainted. Two or three more passed out during the period, and were allowed to stay on the floor. Naismith explained that fainting was nature's way of getting the blood back to a person's head by getting the head as low or lower than the heart. In a short time each student recovered and sheepishly regained his chair. The class learned two lessons that day.

Shenk also told a story about a class Naismith was teaching on tumbling, in which students were diving over a horse onto a pile of mats. "A football player with little tumbling experience asked, 'Doc, how do I land?' Doc's reply was 'Gravity will take care of that.' No one laughed harder than Naismith when the student hit on his head and got up ruefully rubbing his neck."

Another time, toward the end of the semester, Naismith informed his kinesiology class that the next class session would be a picnic. One of the students lived on a farm at the edge of town and provided baked chickens for the lunch. "The catch was that each person receiving a piece of chicken had to identify the major muscles and their origin, insertion and blood supply before eating his piece of chicken," Shenk said. "Many class members have never liked chicken as well since that affair."

Another student recalled an incident in Naismith's course on "Health and First Aid." The student, Max Moxley, was a reporter on the student newspaper, and his work in the newsroom frequently made him late to Naismith's class, which was held in a lecture hall. "A sort of deception to cover the tardy pupil was devised," Paul Long wrote in a story about Naismith included in the Kansas archives. "When Moxley was late and Dr. Naismith called the roll, some classmate from his frat house would answer for him. One day Moxley got to class late and Dr. Naismith was lecturing. As Max entered the classroom in old Robinson Gymnasium, Dr. Naismith stopped his lecture and asked, 'What's your name?' 'I'm Moxley,' Max answered. Checking down the roll, Dr. Naismith said, 'Go sit down, you're already here.'"

Everyone who knew Naismith's routine knew that he went home for lunch every day, and then he liked to lie down on the couch in his living room for a short nap. Not wanting to bother his wife, he developed his own alarm system to make sure he would not oversleep. Elbel said that Naismith would place a tin pan next to the couch and would "hold his key ring and keys in his outstretched hand, above the pan. When the keys dropped into the pan he'd realize that he was completely relaxed and would get up and walk back to his office."

One of Naismith's greatest interests was the development of the human body, and he frequently conducted research with his students. One survey he took in 1924–1925 concerned the use of various types of tobacco, and at what age the students had begun to use it. He was also concerned with alcohol, as his earlier creation of a form of breathalyzer revealed. That work continued into the 1930s.

When he was working as the team physician for the basketball team, Naismith carried a bottle of brandy in his medical kit. He discovered that if he did not keep a close eye on the kit, the level of the brandy bottle would decrease. Shenk said "he solved the problem by labeling the brandy 'Spiritus Frumentum.' Since the tipplers' ability in Latin did not match their thirst, his brandy was undisturbed after that."

Away from the classroom, Naismith became increasingly interested in the hobby of woodworking. He once made a solid black-walnut sideboard for his dining room out of wood he collected from trees knocked down in a tornado.

With his son Jack's help, Naismith built a new house for his family on Mississippi Street, near the university. Father and son even combined to build another, smaller house on the same street, which the family used as rental property.

Shortly after arriving at Kansas, Naismith had become a charter member of what was known as the Saturday Night Club, an informal group of 12 men that met for dinner and then a discussion. The group first met weekly, but later reduced its gathering to a monthly basis. The forums were a pleasant diversion for Naismith from the troubles he was having at the university. Naismith or one of the other members usually chose a topic for the night's discussion. In the more than 20 years that Naismith participated in the meetings, he chose topics as diverse as motherhood, lumberjacks, politics versus religion, athletes and religion, religious intolerance, the development of character through athletics, and work versus play.

Naismith once said of the club, "There are two facts that are always very much in evidence in this club. 1, that every member feels himself capable of discussing any subject without any preparation; 2, that no question was ever unanimously settled by this crowd. If there are always two sides to a question this bunch always sees the two sides, so that I suppose it is futile to ask you to settle a question."

In a 1934 address to the club, Naismith said, "For 28 years I have been writing papers for the Saturday Night Club, and nearly all of them have been on subjects about which I thought I knew something, but before the evening was over, my fellow club members had almost convinced me that I knew nothing about the question."

Another diversion for the family came when Naismith brought home a new baby goat as a present for his son Jim. They named the goat Jazzbo, and he immediately made his presence known.

The goat jumped on the railing of the back porch and went for a stroll, calmly knocking over the milk bottles that were sunning on the rail, sending them crashing onto the concrete patio below.

One day while Jim was at school, Jazzbo went for a stroll and happened to stop on the streetcar tracks. The driver rang his bell, but Jazzbo wouldn't move. The driver got off his streetcar to try to chase Jazzbo away, but instead Jazzbo charged toward him. The driver climbed back onto the streetcar, and the two squared off again. Finally the ringing of the bell and everyone's yells attracted the police, who were dispatched to the school to get Jim to move Jazzbo off the tracks so the streetcar service could resume.

Naismith was amused by Jazzbo, and he helped exercise the pet by holding a rag on a stick while Jazzbo ran at it. One day, when Naismith turned his back toward Jazzbo to bend over and pick up the rag, the goat rammed him, sending Naismith sprawling onto the ground. Not long after, Naismith decided to return the goat to the milkman's farm from which he had come.

Such diversions helped keep Naismith from worrying about his changing role at the university. He also had to deal with another personal loss when he received word that his sister, Annie, had died in Canada in 1929. Never married, she had spent her adult life taking care of her uncle Peter, who had raised Annie and James after the deaths of their parents. Naismith also mourned the death of his uncle Peter three years later.

Like the rest of the country, Naismith and his family were affected by the Great Depression after the stock market collapse in 1929. The university began to cut the salaries of faculty members, and Naismith—who had never worried about finances—fell behind on his mortgage payments. Between the salary reductions at the university and the loss of summer income, Naismith's income was cut by almost $1,000, about a 25 percent drop.

The bank was preparing to foreclose on the house when Phog Allen heard about the situation. Allen went to Naismith and asked if what he had heard was true, and Naismith admitted it was. Allen then asked Naismith if he would like to keep the house, and again Naismith said yes. Allen went to the bank and made arrangements to allow Naismith to stay in the house.

Naismith decided to talk about the situation with his wife and son Jack, who was the only one of the five children still living at home. The family decided they didn't really need the big house, so they let the bank have the building, and they moved into the smaller home down the street that they had been using as rental property.

The move didn't really worry Naismith. A friend reported that he ran into Naismith on the sidewalk as the family was in the process of moving. He was walking with a military stride, carrying a rifle on his shoulder—and the clothes from his closet on hangers attached to the rifle barrel.

Much more upsetting to Naismith was the news that five people, including members of the Canadian national AAU champion basketball team, the Winnipeg Toilers, had been killed in a plane crash near Neodesha, Kansas, on March 31, 1933. Naismith was very fond of the team and had accepted an invitation to speak to the team members before they played a three-game exhibition series against a team from Tulsa, Oklahoma, the U.S. champions, in Tulsa. At the time the series was billed as the first international championship contest in the history of basketball. Naismith and his son Jack drove to Tulsa and watched as the Winnipeg team lost to the Tulsa Oilers. Two days later, he was in Wichita when he received the news about the plane crash. Colonel A. C. Sampson, one of the team's sponsors, was injured in the accident. Naismith and his son went to the scene of the crash, then on to the hospital where the injured were being treated.

"On arriving at the hospital I was ushered into the room of Col. Sampson," Naismith wrote. "I will never forget the sight that met my eyes. Here was a man that had gone through a wreck that claimed several lives and he looked up and greeted me with a smile.

"That attitude that both Col. Sampson and the players on that Toilers' team displayed will always cause me to think of that group as some of the finest sportsmen that I have ever met."

Ironically, the crash came two years to the day after another plane crash in Kansas, about 100 miles away, had killed eight people, including the famed Notre Dame football coach Knute Rockne, who was a personal friend of Naismith's and had been a guest in Naismith's home many times.

Those tragedies reminded Naismith that there was no reason to be concerned about smaller, trivial matters, such as not having any money. He also never let himself be concerned by what others perceived as a lack of recognition—even what could have been viewed as disrespect—for his role in inventing basketball. One honor he did receive, and shared with his good friends Amos Alonzo Stagg and R. Tait McKenzie, was the Honor Award of Fellow in Physical Education by the American Association of Health, Physical Education and Recreation in 1931. When Miss Mable Lee presented the award, she said, "Dr. Naismith had a vision, far ahead of his time, of the social values of recreative and competitive athletics and he deserted the ministry, for which he had spent a number of years in preparation, because he saw the great opportunity in recreative physical education for character training of boys and young men."

Naismith saw another opportunity to make a contribution to society when a student named John McLendon walked into his office one day in the fall of 1933.

• • •

CHAPTER 11

Becoming a Mentor

John McLendon graduated from Sumner High School in Kansas City. He loved basketball and had decided as early as the sixth grade that he wanted to become a coach. He wanted to attend college in Springfield, Massachusetts, but could not afford to go that far away. McLendon's father told him that the man who had invented the game was teaching just down the road in Lawrence, and "I ought to go there and learn from him."

Furthermore, when McLendon's father dropped him off at Kansas, he told his son to go find Naismith and introduce himself: "Tell him that he's to be your adviser." McLendon found the office, knocked on the door and went inside, and did exactly as his father had told him to do. Naismith responded by saying, "Who told you to do this?"

McLendon answered, "My father," and Naismith said, "Fathers are always right."

Thus began a relationship between McLendon and Naismith that was to last the rest of Naismith's life and prove instrumental to McLendon's future coaching success. There is one additional detail, however, that cannot be overlooked: McLendon was black.

A special act by the Kansas state legislature had allowed Naismith to remain on the university faculty past the mandatory retirement age of 70. He was told he could teach as long as he wanted, and the required class in health education that he taught to all freshmen remained one of the school's most popular classes.

McLendon recalled years later, in an interview with the *New York Times*, a conversation between Naismith and the dean of the school, who wanted Naismith to explain why so many students were receiving As in the class. Naismith reportedly said, "Anybody that came to my class deserved a good grade if they had to listen to me."

When he arrived at Kansas, McLendon was one of only seven students majoring in physical education at the university and one of only 60 black students in a population of about 4,000 overall. "Many of my doubts about being at Kansas were quickly dispelled by Dr. Naismith, who treated me courteously and attentively, and made me feel comfortable in my surroundings as a new student," McLendon told the *Times* in 1996.

Naismith had strong feelings against segregation, which dated back to his time working with the military along the Mexican border and then in World War I in France. He had spoken often with black soldiers, and he talked about how much he enjoyed and benefited from the experience. While the Naismith family did employ a black woman, known as Auntie Silvers, to help with household chores and child care, Naismith viewed her as another member of the family and never as a servant. He also would not allow his children to view her as less than their equal.

Still, McLendon's arrival on campus presented Naismith with a new challenge because there were many people at the university who had strong feelings against blacks in general and black students in particular.

"Dr. Naismith didn't know anything about color or nationality," McLendon said in an interview with *Kansas Alumni* magazine in 1979. "He was so unconscious about your economic or religious background. He just saw everyone as potential. There wasn't anything in his body that responded to anything racist."

McLendon found that wasn't the case among other university personnel, however. "I walked out of one class because the teacher continued to tell ethnic jokes," he said in the same interview. "I had to go back, because the course was required. It was the only 'C' I ever got in my years at KU."

Another time, McLendon dropped a class because the teacher accused him of cheating, and he knew the only reason for that accusation was that he was black.

At that time, all students were required to pass a swimming and water safety course before they could graduate. The problem for black students was that, because of the segregation rules, they were not allowed to use the school's swimming pool. Instead, they were automatically given passing grades without ever taking the course. McLendon, backed by Naismith, objected.

"I refused to go along," McLendon said. "To give blacks automatic grades wasn't fair to the students taking the class, and the matter of water safety, being able to swim and to know water safety, was just too important.

"I got Dr. Naismith to go with me to Dr. Allen, and I asked him if we could make a deal. I asked him to open up the pool to everyone for two weeks, and, if there was no trouble, to keep it open for everybody all the time. He agreed."

Without either Naismith's or Allen's knowledge, McLendon then called a meeting of all 60 black students and told them to avoid the pool for the next two weeks, which they agreed to do. When no incidents were reported, Allen kept his promise to keep the pool open to all students.

One rumor spread that after McLendon took and passed the required swimming test, the pool was drained. McLendon said it wasn't true. Only half the pool was drained, he said, at which point he reminded the officials how much it was going to cost if they drained the pool completely and then had to refill it. The workers instead refilled the pool.

McLendon, who had not been allowed to play basketball in junior high or high school because he was black, never played the sport at Kansas either, but he learned a great deal about it from his work with Naismith. McLendon took classes from Naismith in physical education, anatomy, and kinesiology. He joked that the students "always tried to get him off the subject of anatomy," usually by asking a question about basketball.

"Dr. Naismith taught me far more than was found in textbooks," McLendon said in the *Times* interview. "Very often he would put aside his books and teach us lessons in life from his world experiences.

"He was an inventive teacher. He would take our class out on the highway, a long stretch of flat road on the Kansas plains. There he would conduct an experiment to show us how to measure the kinesthetic sense of an individual and how it could be a predictor of physical skill. The method he used was to have us drive a car at about 35 miles per hour and then try to eliminate various factors like vibration, sight, feeling and hearing while we were driving the car, to test our kinesthetic sense. If you could sustain the speed of the car at 35 miles per hour while blindfolded, with your ears clogged or sitting inside an inner tube, according to Dr. Naismith, you had great kinesthetic sense as an athlete."

Naismith provided McLendon with his greatest aid when it came time for McLendon to complete another portion of the work required to earn his degree—a student teaching assignment. "As the first black physical education student enrolled in the school, it would be difficult for me to teach white students at segregated schools, so I was to be excused from practice teaching," McLendon recalled. "When I told Dr. Naismith about my problem, he told me to come back in a day or two and he might have an answer."

Indeed, Naismith did come up with a plan for McLendon. Even though McLendon was a junior, Naismith assigned him to begin student teaching then instead of during his senior year, which was the customary practice. He also told McLendon that he was going to experience teaching physical education at the elementary, middle school, and high school level, in both segregated and integrated classes.

Naismith assigned McLendon to Lincoln Elementary School, a segregated school in Lawrence. At the same time, he also told McLendon to report to Lawrence Junior High, which was integrated, to teach gymnastics. Later that year, he moved McLendon to Lawrence High School, an integrated school but with separate white and black boy's basketball teams, where McLendon would work as an assistant basketball coach.

By the next year, McLendon was named the head coach of the high school's black team, and the team won the Kansas-Missouri Athletic Conference championship. After watching McLendon coach, Naismith told him, "Whatever you do in physical education, stick with this game."

McLendon did as he was told. "He was the man in my life," he said of Naismith. "He taught me everything I know about basketball and physical education. Everything I ever did when I was coaching, I can trace back to learning it from him.

"I learned my philosophy of coaching. . . . He told me never to put X's and O's on a chalkboard. It was more important to instill positive thinking and good orientation to let your players know their long- and short-range objectives and to build your program step by step.

"He always used to say the ultimate goal of basketball was to attack wherever the opponent got the ball, and to start the offense whenever and wherever you got the ball. From this came the full-court press and the fast-break offense. I built my whole coaching career around this."

When he graduated in 1936, McLendon was eager to begin coaching full time, but once again he listened to Naismith's advice. Naismith called a friend at the University of Iowa and told him he had a student with great potential who needed a job, and by the time he hung up the phone, McLendon was working in Iowa's research department so he could continue his education at that school.

McLendon did go on to coach, and proved very successful at his chosen profession. In his 25 years of coaching, McLendon's teams won more than 650 games and compiled a nearly .800 winning percentage. He coached Tennessee State to three consecutive National Association of Intercollegiate Athletics (NAIA) championships in 1957, 1958, and 1959. He also coached on the collegiate level at North Carolina College, Hampton Institute, Kentucky State, and Cleveland State.

He became the first black to work as a head coach in professional basketball, with the Cleveland Pipers of the American Basketball League, and he later was the head coach of the Denver Rockets of the American Basketball Association. He was also the first black appointed to the U.S. Olympic Basketball Committee, and he was elected to the Naismith Memorial Basketball Hall of Fame in 1979.

McLendon knew none of that would have been possible except for the guidance and assistance he received from Naismith. "He was such a busy man, but he always found time to help students," McLendon said. "I guess that because he was my adviser, he gave me a little extra help. He knew that I was greatly interested in administration, and he would give me bits and pieces, insights on how he did things.

"There's no question that my life would not have been anywhere near what it has become if I had not had Dr. Naismith as my adviser. He never looked at life as black and white. One thing he taught . . . was that no matter what kind of problem you had, never let it defeat you. Even though you may not think something is fair or just, you can't let that stop you. You just try to get around it. . . . His philosophy was that adversity is just another opportunity."

That was true with McLendon, and it was true as well with another student who came through Kansas in the early 1930s—a track star named Glenn Cunningham.

When Cunningham was seven years old, in his hometown of Elkhart, Kansas, his legs were severely burned in a schoolhouse explosion and fire that killed his brother. Doctors wanted to amputate both legs, and they warned that even if they were able to save his legs, he would probably never walk again.

Cunningham didn't listen to that prognosis. After the doctors did save his legs, he devoted himself to proving them wrong, and after a year of strenuous exercise he learned to walk again. Then, miraculously, he began to run. He became a high school track star and brought his talent with him to Lawrence.

Naismith knew the young man's background and was fascinated by the story because of his interest in working with crippled persons and others who had lost the use of their limbs through injuries. Even though Cunningham had fully recovered from his injuries before he met Naismith, the two spent many hours discussing how Cunningham had been able to prove his doctors wrong.

Naismith could not resist giving Cunningham a piece of advice when he overheard the young man giving pointers about endurance to some of his fellow track team members. Cunningham was describing how he found a "second wind" when he was running. "You'll kill those boys," Naismith reportedly said. "They don't have your heart."

When Cunningham led Kansas to the Big Six track championship in 1931, Naismith was among the pleased fans. That was only the beginning of Cunningham's accomplishments, however. He finished fourth in the 1,500 meters at the 1932 Olympics, and then set world records for the mile run, both indoors and outdoors, in 1934. He also set a world record for the 1,500 meters at an AAU event that year in New York. In addition, he ran the fastest 800 meters in the world.

With Naismith in attendance at the 1936 Olympics in Berlin, Cunningham finished second in the 1,500 meters, earning the silver medal.

Naismith, of course, was really in Berlin for another reason—receiving credit and recognition as the sport of basketball, his invention, was added to the roster of Olympic sports.

• • •

CHAPTER 12

Olympic Pride

Even though basketball had been played in the Olympics as far back as the 1904 Games in St. Louis, those contests had always been viewed as "exhibitions" or a "demonstration" because teams from only one country participated. Similar contests were played at the 1924 Olympics in Paris and at the 1928 Games in Amsterdam.

By the 1930s, however, basketball definitely had grown to become an international sport. The sport was being played competitively in more than 20 countries on the continents of North America, South America, Europe, Asia, and Africa.

Phog Allen had campaigned to have the sport included at the 1932 Games in Los Angeles, but did not have enough support to get that goal accomplished. He then began to work toward having the sport added for the 1936 Olympics in Berlin, and this time he was successful.

With the sport added to the roster, Allen came up with another idea—he wanted to have Naismith and his wife Maude attend the Games as special guests of honor, so that Naismith could be saluted for his invention of the sport. Allen took his idea to the National Association of Basketball Coaches, and they endorsed the plan. The leading supporters were Allen and A. C. "Dutch" Lonborg, a former Kansas athlete (and the school's future athletic director) who was then the coach at Northwestern. The association designated the week of February 9–15, 1936, as "Naismith Week," and the plan called for one penny to be set aside from every ticket sold to a basketball game anywhere in the United States that week. Those pennies, collected in a fund, would pay for the Naismiths' travel to Berlin, and if any money was available after the trip expenses were paid, it would be used to create another type of memorial.

While the original concept was for money to be collected from college and high school games, the campaign spread to include professional games, church league games, youth league games— anywhere that someone was willing to organize the effort. The campaign even spread to Naismith's native Canada, where $20 was collected at a high school game in Almonte.

The honor of making the first contribution to the fund went to Lawrence High School, which collected money when it played Ottawa, Kansas, High School in late January. A crowd of 515 spectators turned out, and at halftime more money was raised when members of the school's pep squad stretched out blankets and had fans throw change onto the blankets. After the school collected more money throughout the week, a newspaper headline reported that $51.40 had been raised for the fund.

AAU teams in Kansas and Missouri also contributed to the fund, with $31.34 being raised at a game between Santa Fe Trails and Philco in Kansas City. A KU graduate who had moved to Oklahoma, Robert K. Johnston, sent in an individual contribution of $25. The Gridleys, an independent team in Wichita, donated $52.58 to the fund. The largest contribution from a single game, not surprisingly, came from the Kansas–Kansas State game in Lawrence on February 16, when $105.35 was raised.

Before that game, Chancellor Ernest Lindley, the man who had replaced Naismith as the director of physical education and given the job to Allen, praised Naismith by saying that "he is a man whose influence has gone further than that of any other man in Kansas."

Kansas high schools combined to contribute $550 to the fund, and the total of more than $1,000 raised in Kansas was the most collected in any state. Overall, with contributions coming from 43 states and Canada, the amount raised exceeded $5,000, and this was more than enough to fund the trip.

Before leaving for the Olympics, Naismith received two more honors. He was invited to be the guest of honor at the AAU national tournament in Denver, where the top two teams would earn bids to the Olympic Trials in New York. Naismith was also invited to that tournament, where the team representing the United States in the Olympics would be selected.

Naismith was pleased that one of the two teams to make the AAU finals turned out to be the McPherson Oilers, from McPherson, Kansas. The Oilers won the AAU tournament by defeating the Universal Pictures team from Hollywood, California.

Both teams qualified for the Olympic Trials. At the time, entire teams qualified for the Trials, not just individuals. Five colleges earned berths in the Trials, where they were joined by the two AAU teams and a YMCA team from Wilmerding, Pennsylvania. The Wilmerding team had lost the YMCA national tournament to a team from Denver, but it was later determined that the Denver team had also competed in the AAU tournament, and for that reason Denver was disqualified.

Naismith and Phog Allen were disappointed that the Kansas team was not one of the five college teams to earn spots in the Trials. The five were the University of Washington, the University of Arkansas, DePaul University, Utah State University, and Temple University. Kansas had gone 18–0 in the regular season, then defeated Washburn and Oklahoma State, setting up a best-of-three series against Utah State, in Kansas City, to determine a spot in the Olympic Trials. The Kansas Jayhawks won the first game, 39–37 in overtime, and needed to win just one of the two remaining games to earn the trip to New York. Instead, Utah

State won both games, 42–37 and 50–31, earning the spot in the Trials.

The two defeats cost Allen the chance to be the coach of the Olympic team, but he still was scheduled to work as a director of the Olympic Basketball Committee. That position, however, did not last long.

One of the differences of opinion between Naismith and Allen concerned the participation of AAU teams in the Trials. While Naismith wholeheartedly endorsed their participation, Allen did not approve of the selections, thinking only college teams should earn positions in the Trials. Allen became even more upset when he found out that the money from the National Collegiate Athletic Association (NCAA) district qualifying tournament in Kansas City, which he had run, was going to the AAU. He turned in his letter of resignation to the Olympic Committee and did not travel to Berlin for the Games.

The rules at the time called for whichever team won the Trials to be awarded seven spots on the U.S. team's roster for the Olympics, with the second-place team earning five spots. The final two players on the 14-man roster were to be selected from the other six teams. The coach was to come from the winning team, with the losing coach from the finals to work as his assistant.

The Trials were held at Madison Square Garden, and a crowd of 12,000 fans showed up for the first round, a series of four games that lasted more than six hours. Naismith officially opened the tournament, and he confessed in an interview that he was enjoying himself immensely. "The boys certainly are treating me royally," he told a United Press reporter. "It will be the thrill of my life when we sail for the Olympic Games. And of course I'm getting a huge kick of coming here to see the first American Olympic finals. I'm more pleased and excited than a farmboy at his first circus."

The Trials were a single-elimination format, and the two AAU teams emerged as the finalists over the college teams and the YMCA team. McPherson, having just defeated the Universal Pictures team two weeks earlier in Denver, was a huge favorite to win. The result was an upset, however, with the Universal team winning by one point to earn the most spots on the Olympic roster.

Naismith went back to Lawrence even more excited about the upcoming trip, if that was possible. The Olympics were considered the greatest athletic event in the world, and they were a tribute to amateur athletes, representing the ideals and values that Naismith cherished.

Despite his differences with Allen, Naismith knew it was Allen's leadership of the fundraising campaign that had allowed him and Maude to plan their trip to Europe. His friend Edwin Elbel had drawn a sketch of Naismith and had several copies made. Naismith gave one to Allen, inscribing it, "With kindest regards to Dr. F. C. Allen, the father of basketball coaching, from the father of the game, James Naismith." Allen had the picture framed and proudly hung it on the wall of his office.

Naismith thought the upcoming trip would be like a second honeymoon for him and Maude. When he was finishing his work with the YMCA in France at the end of World War I, he had tried unsuccessfully to talk her into coming to visit him there, or at least coming to meet him in Scotland, but she had refused.

Naismith no doubt knew that having his sport included in the Olympics truly showed it was an international game, even though he personally considered that it had earned that status from the very first game ever played on December 21, 1891, at Springfield. Players in that first game had included four Canadians, three Americans, and an Englishman. Also in the class were a student from Japan and another from France. Having the game displayed for all the world to see, however, was an event of far greater magnitude.

There was more heartache to come for Naismith, however, before he could enjoy his moment of glory in Berlin. Only a few days before he and Maude planned to leave for New York, from where they were to sail across the Atlantic, Maude suffered a heart attack. The doctors assured Naismith that she would recover, but thought the trip would be too much for her. He reluctantly agreed and decided to take her to Dallas, where she could be cared for by their daughter Hellen and son James while he was overseas.

Naismith traveled by train from Dallas to New York, where he boarded the ship *Samaria* for an eight-day voyage across the ocean to Glasgow, Scotland, the first stop on his European tour. As he had done the first time he crossed the Atlantic 19 years earlier, he wrote to Maude to describe his trip.

"Life on board ship is a pretty monotonous affair unless you feel extra good and want to gab about nothing," he wrote. "Last night we had a cabaret in the dining room and an Episcopal minister made a joke about the Catholics and there were plenty of them there, then to straighten things out he said that if he were not an Episcopal, he would be a Catholic, then all the other denominations booed him. I have not seen him on deck or in the lounge since, I guess he hunted a hole to hide in. I am keeping quiet. I may be uninteresting but do not make that kind of a fool of myself."

In addition to his letters home, Naismith kept a journal while on his trip. The most interesting event he saw while in Glasgow was greyhound racing. He even included a diagram of the track in his notes and commented, "I don't know what is going on but I guess they do."

After stopping in Edinburgh, Naismith was on his way to London. He wrote to Maude on July 25: "This is Saturday night and I have had a strenuous week. This morning I took a sightseeing tour. This afternoon I visited the British Museum, the University and the YMCA. This evening I went to a show and then strutted around to some of the 'pubs' and saw some sights that make me more than ever a teetotaler. There were women 50 years of age whopping it up drunk as Lords, then younger women, then children from little Don's age to little Hellen's, with people who were probably their parents drinking, and they were hanging around getting the leavings."

In his diary, Naismith noted that he was disappointed by his trip to the London YMCA, saying he "got very little out of it." Yet that didn't appear to concern him as much as his upcoming trip through Denmark and Belgium, on his way to Berlin. In a letter to Maude dated July 28, Naismith wrote, "I do not know how I will get along when I can't ask for something to eat but will not starve if I have to point to what I want. If I can't get to my hotel at least I can write the name, even if I can't pronounce it. I will be able to get along once I reach France."

Naismith noted in his diary that he went out to eat at a restaurant in Brussels. "When I asked for something to eat he sent me to the back of the room and I waited 15 minutes and then had to hail a waiter," he wrote. "The meal: tomato soup, fried sole, roast pork, cup of tea . . . 19 francs, 57 cents."

By August 1, Naismith had finally made it to Berlin, just as the Olympic ceremonies were getting underway.

There was a lot of uncertainty around the world about how well the Games would fare. The selection of Berlin as the host city had been made by the Olympic committee five years earlier, before the Nazi party and Adolf Hitler came to power in Germany. One of the major concerns was how the black and Jewish athletes would be treated.

In Berlin, and in Germany as a whole, the citizens viewed the Olympics as a chance to display their national pride. The country had built a grand new stadium on a 325-acre plot of ground, seating 100,000 spectators. Every seat was filled for the opening ceremonies on a gray and rainy day, and Hitler was there to welcome the 5,000 athletes and officially open the Games. The color and pageantry of the Olympics filled the city, a fact that Naismith and others mentioned often.

Hitler was not a sports fan, preferring the opera and long mountain walks as his forms of entertainment and relaxation. He had not been expected to attend any of the competitions once the Olympics started, but one day he decided to watch the track and field events since he had never before seen that competition. He was immediately hooked, and from that day on attended as many Olympic events as possible, except when government business kept him occupied.

Hitler had hoped to use the Olympics as proof of the superiority of the Aryan race, but he had to watch black American Jesse Owens win four gold medals in the track events, no doubt a sour moment for Hitler. His goal of using the Games to spread the word about Nazi power was working, however, as he or other government officials hosted parties almost every night, inviting officials from the competing countries. It has been reported that Naismith was invited and attended one of those parties, but he never made any references to the evening in a letter to his wife or in his diary, so the Nazi influence was apparently of little concern to him.

Naismith did have other matters that captured his attention. He was disappointed to learn that no special ceremony had been arranged for the opening of the basketball competition. Even worse, he was initially denied entrance to the Games because his name had somehow been removed from the pass list. He was admitted only after some quick work by friends and other officials with the U.S. delegation.

Other problems developed, too, but they were more of a concern for the coach of the U.S. team, James Needles, and the players. After arriving in Berlin, they learned that some of the rules they were accustomed to would not be followed in the Games. There would be no three-second violation (a rule initiated a few years earlier to try to eliminate stalling), the teams would be limited to seven players, and the games would be played on an outdoor court covered with a combination of sand, sawdust, and salt. One proposed rule change that the United States was able to overturn would have barred players 6'2" or taller from competing—and at least six of the U.S. players were that height or taller.

Because the United States had brought a 14-player roster, it was decided that the squad would be split in half and the two teams would alternate games.

In his letters home and in his diary, Naismith made little reference to these problems. He concentrated instead on comments about the citizens and the city:

> The women and girls are serious, they do not smile like our girls or show their teeth. No paint or powder. The girls are told to leave it off if they travel the streets.
>
> The shops are beautiful, the window displays excellent. The number of different uniforms is immense, soldiers of all classes. There is one group of boys all speaking English, and they are very courteous. They do not seem to expect tips and all are as kind as they can be. . . . There are bands of girls marching the streets singing their songs. Most of the street music has a marching swing and it is accented just right.
>
> In the stadium there is a tower about 30 feet high for the camera. The track and places for the jump are beautifully laid out and every detail is attended to with minuteness. Man goes in and takes his seat, wife follows after. Man sits down in restaurant, woman gets own seat.

After officials realized that nothing special had been planned to honor Naismith, a version of the Olympic opening ceremony was arranged for the nations competing in basketball before that competition began. Naismith stood proudly on August 7 as members of teams representing 21 countries strolled past him, the most countries participating in any of the team sports at the Berlin games. Originally 22 countries had been entered in the basketball competition, but the team from Spain had been called home after civil war broke out in that country. Naismith acknowledged the greetings of the teams in a speech.

Naismith confessed later that, as he was greeted by cheers from each of the foreign delegations, tears came to his eyes. It was, he recalled later, the single greatest moment of his life, and it was then that he more accurately realized what his invention of the game of basketball just 45 years earlier already meant to the world.

"As he watched the boys dressed in their suits, each team carrying the flag of its country, stop in front of the reviewing stand and cheer him, his heart swelled and his eyes were filled with tears," his daughter Hellen wrote.

Ever since his days in the seminary, when Naismith knew his goal in life was "to make the world a little better than I found it," all of his efforts had been directed toward that goal. Standing in front of those Olympic basketball players, from every corner of the world, he realized his goal had been accomplished simply with the invention of the sport.

"He blinked several times as the teams passing before him came into focus," Hellen wrote. "These boys were not all the same size nor the same color. They didn't even speak the same language, but they all had one thing in common—basketball, his game."

One fact that made Naismith beam even brighter was the knowledge that the coaching staffs of the competing nations included 17 graduates of the YMCA Training School (by then known as the International YMCA College) who had taken the game—his game—with them as they traveled to those countries.

Naismith had the honor of tossing up the first ball at the opening game, between Estonia and France. "He stepped back to his seat and sat for a moment with bowed head," Hellen wrote. "He knew the meaning of 'my cup runneth over.' He knew in this moment that his prayers uttered so long ago had indeed been answered and that he had given something to the world that would bring all nations a little closer together and make the world a little better place in which to live."

Naismith knew this was true when the luck of the first-round draw paired China and Japan, two countries very much aware of their political differences, and the game went off without any disputes.

The United States won its first game by forfeit, 2–0, over the missing Spanish team. The United States then defeated Estonia, 52–28, and the Philippines, 56–23, to move into the medal round. Naismith noted in his diary that if the U.S. team had not enjoyed a height advantage over the Philippines, the Philippines might have won the game. He also wrote, "crowd in fervor."

The United States then played Mexico, winning 25–10 to set up the gold medal game against Canada. Naismith could not have been more pleased at the results—the country of his birth playing the country of his choice for the championship.

The games were played outdoors, on an unpaved court, but there were no provisions for weather problems. The championship game was played in a driving rain, even though there was an empty gymnasium nearby. There were no seats for spectators, so the crowd estimated at 1,000 had to stand through the entire game, won by the United States by the score of 19–8. The weather conditions played a major role in the low score, as players were unable to control the ball by dribbling it. Joe Fortenbury led the U.S. team with seven points. Naismith congratulated the victorious players and presented them with their gold medals.

He reflected later that one of the reasons he was so pleased with the final game was that the referee was from China, and "there was not a single questioning of his rulings."

A KU graduate student, W. H. Mifflin, was with Naismith that afternoon and recalled the event nearly 50 years later in a letter to the *Kansas Alumni* magazine: "I was a guest of Dr. Naismith and what a thrill it was for him to see the game," Mifflin wrote. "After the game, Dr. Naismith and I had walked a short distance and were stopped by two German girls of Hitler's organization. They put two wreaths of flowers around Dr. Naismith's neck, bowed and left.

"I made the remark to Dr. Naismith about the results of the game, 'Doctor this should be the crowning event of your life. What an honor.' He replied, 'Billie, it is.'"

In his final letter home before leaving Berlin, Naismith reflected on the events and activities of the previous two weeks: "I certainly have had a wonderful time and have made a world of friends from every part of this planet, and have had my picture snapped with every team. Most of them want a picture of me standing with the coach and manager. . . . I made friends with a German guard and he became my personal bodyguard. Seated me in the best places at the basketball games and though he could not speak English and I could not speak German, we got along nicely by signs and a few German words that I picked up. I have learned to get my dinner from a German menu and that is some job."

Naismith wasn't quite ready to begin his journey home. He had more appointments in Switzerland, where he again was honored as the inventor of the game. He returned by way of Canada, visiting relatives, before arriving back in Lawrence in mid-September, two months after he had left.

Even though the addition of basketball to the Olympics was the greatest achievement of his life, Naismith never had been content to live in the past. He didn't know then that there would be no Olympics in either 1940 or 1944 because of World War II. He was now 75 years old, but he was looking to the future as he came back home.

CHAPTER 13

The Changing Game

One of the reasons Naismith had such an enjoyable time at the Olympics basketball competition was that the rules used for the games were the older, more traditional ones, without some of the new rules that had been put in place for games in the United States during the previous seasons.

Specifically, the Olympics retained the "old" rules of not having a center line and not forcing teams to move the ball across that line within 10 seconds. The rules also kept the center jump rule after a free throw was made.

Naismith said many times that he was not opposed to changes in the rules of "his" game, and he said repeatedly that as the athletes became more experienced, the skill level of the players was increasing. He did not approve of all of the changes, however, and the two he resisted the most were the 10-second rule and the elimination of the center jump. His most quoted comment was, "Don't get too far away from the original game. It was the best game."

The 10-second rule was a source of disagreement between Naismith and Phog Allen. In fact, one day while Allen was telling reporters at Robinson Gym all of the reasons why he favored the new rule, Naismith was in his office on a different floor, preparing a statement about why he adamantly opposed the rule change.

The change was designed to keep teams from "stalling" because it forced them to bring the ball across the half-court line within 10 seconds. It came about after teams started using the "five-man defense," with every player trying to keep the other team from scoring. There was no provision in the rules, however, about how long a team could continue to hold the ball once it was across half court.

"The crowds were not attending the games as they had, and the players were not as enthusiastic as they had been before," Naismith wrote. "Something had to be done. At this point, a few men who were exponents of the five-man defense made a great cry about the harm of stalling. Through newspaper propaganda, the spectators were led to believe that the team in possession of the ball was doing the stalling, and for some time when the offensive team refused to enter a closely set defense, the crowd would boo and accuse them of stalling.

"It is my contention, and that of many coaches with whom I have talked, that when this condition occurs, the blame should be placed on the team that does not attempt to get the ball. . . . Some teams, when on the defense, had clustered around the basket and remained in this position for 19 minutes, making no advance toward the ball. Under these conditions the people were forced to sit in their seats and watch 10 men on the floor doing nothing. A great many people did not care to pay to see two teams at opposite ends of the floor looking at each other."

A meeting of coaches was held in 1932, and even though Naismith did not attend, he submitted a couple of suggestions that he thought would help eliminate the problem. His first suggestion was that any defensive team that retreated under the basket and did not make an attempt to get the ball within 30 seconds should be penalized and the other team awarded a free throw. In essence, Naismith was proposing a shot clock, although he again was putting the pressure on the defense to try to get the ball instead of on the offense to try to score.

Second, Naismith suggested that any basket from outside of the defensive perimeter should count for four points instead of the normal two for a field goal. Again, he was ahead of his time. It was not until 1979 that the three-point shot was adopted by the National Basketball Association, and the NCAA did not institute the three-point shot until 1986.

Instead, the coaches voted to enact the 10-second rule. Naismith was upset and predicted the rule would not stop stalling. He later pointed to a game in the 1934 national tournament when the Stage Liners crossed the center court line and then held the ball for 12 minutes without attempting to score. He said the team made 343 passes during those 12 minutes.

"This clamor for 'more scoring' is not so much that the spectators want the ball actually going through the basket as it is a desire for more spirited action," Naismith said. "Didn't you ever notice how the crowd goes wild when a player by skillful play intercepts a ball intended for an opponent, or by clever plays takes the ball from an inattentive opponent?"

The other rule change that Naismith strongly opposed was the elimination of the center jump. He tried to convince the coaches who opposed the center jump that "it originally was designed to give each team an equal chance to get the ball, and the team with the better jumper had the advantage." He attempted to prove his point that there was more skill involved in winning the center jump than merely which team had the taller player:

"In a class in kinesiology, the question of judgment versus height was brought up," Naismith wrote. "In order to satisfy the members of the class, two basketball players were selected, one four inches taller than the other. A basketball was obtained, and we went out on the gymnasium floor. I tossed the ball between them, each time just above the point which the taller man could reach, and without exception the taller man gained the tip.

"Next I tossed the ball considerably higher, and under these conditions the shorter man was able to gain the top an equal number of times. The next step was to toss the ball high and at different heights each time, and under these conditions the shorter man had a decided advantage in the number of tips received. I was convinced that this high toss at varying heights would largely overcome the advantage gained by height alone.

"Personally I feel that the center jump is to basketball what the kickoff is to football. To award the ball to a team after a goal is scored takes away much of the thrill that is present in an opening play. A crowd does not rise to its feet in excitement at the start of a play when the ball is simply given to a team."

The coaches and rules committee listened to Naismith's objections, but then voted to eliminate the center jump except at the start of each half.

Writing in 1938, Naismith explained: "One of the reasons I am sorry to see the center jump relegated to its subordinate place is that it is going to take from the game one of the large elements of suspense. Now suspense is desirable in any sport. Which, do you think, appeals to the spectator more—the actual dropping of the ball through the basket, or the suspense, the seconds wondering if the ball is going in? In the same way, there is suspense in the center jump, and some pretty plays have been built about the uncertainty there."

Not shy about his opposition to the changes in the rules, Naismith spoke out whenever he was given a forum. On a trip to Canada in the spring of 1939, he pointed out how the changes in the rules, designed to speed up the game, had in fact slowed the game down. "Nowadays, just because a rule is new it is thought that it must be good and old rules are sneered at," Naismith said. "From what I have heard in this country, you people are playing the game more nearly as it should be played."

He insisted that he was not opposed to new rules because they were different from his original 13 rules, but because he thought they would prove detrimental to the game. "I am for anything that will improve the game," he said. "However, I don't feel that the recent abolition of the center jump has improved the game, and I dislike, too, the fact that the change was made, and now the burden of unseating it is put on the followers of the established game. Two of the principal advantages urged by proponents of the change, as I gather it, are that abolition of the center jump cures certain ills of over-emphasis on extra tall centers, and that it speeds up the game."

Not ready to concede that he had lost the battle, Naismith made three suggestions, which he thought would overcome coaches' objections to retaining the center jump. He suggested that the official toss the ball higher, as he had during the experiment in his college class, because that would help negate the advantage of the taller man. He also suggested that players taking the center jump be rotated so that the same person would not always take the jump, and third, he suggested that players of no more than a three-inch variance in height be allowed to take the jump. None of his suggestions were approved.

"It would not have been difficult to have tried one of several things to eliminate undue advantage of a tall player, and still have reserved the 'uncertainty' of the jump at center," he said.

There were other ways to get an advantage during the jump, even against taller players, Naismith discovered. He said a former Kansas player, Bill Miller, was constantly able to out-jump a taller player, and Naismith could not merely accept the fact that he was that skilled in jumping. Paying closer attention, Naismith discovered that as the ball was tossed in the air, Miller grabbed the belt of his opponent at the same time that he jumped.

One change that Naismith would have liked to see was the elimination of some of the rough play from the game. Attending a Kansas-Missouri game as far back as 1910, he had commented on the roughness, saying "they are killing my game." He still felt that way in the 1930s. "Fundamentally, I believe the spectators want to see a game that is full of action, and at the same time does not have roughness," he said. "In football, for example, the spectator thrills at the resounding clash of team against team. In basketball, the thrill lies in suspense. The spectator holds his breath as the ball arches through the air; will it score or will it miss the basket?

"One way to get better action and less roughness would be to enforce rule 15 of section 9. Under this rule it is the duty of the player dribbling down the court to make 'an obvious effort' to avoid colliding with a defensive man. All this past season I have noted time after time that the player who maintained his place on the floor, as is his right, has been charged with a foul.

"Another way to lessen roughness would be by returning one of the original rules of the game—the one requiring the ball to be handled by the hands only. When a player hugs the ball to his body, as he does in football, he forces the opponent to unusual exertions to get possession, and roughness inevitably results."

Another way to control roughness, of course, was for the referee working the game to be more diligent in calling fouls. Naismith was quick to point out, however, that it was not the calls of the referee that should determine whether a team won or lost a game. An alternative would be to disqualify a player once he committed two fouls, as was included in the original rules.

"A great many are objecting to games being won by free throws," he said. "If we penalize the offender by taking him out of the game for a length of time, the game would be won by field goals and the player would see the handicap he puts on his team by making fouls, e.g. hockey and lacrosse."

Until those rules were changed again, however, Naismith said it was up to the referee to control the game and call the fouls that should be called. "I firmly believe that the future of basketball lies with the officials," he wrote. "Good officials will make for interesting games and poor officiating destroys the best features of any game, but more especially basketball. I believe that the strict enforcement of rules by a competent, impartial official will develop sportsmanship in the players." These comments remain valid seventy years later.

Naismith was in attendance at an AAU tournament in Kansas City when one of the coaches protested a decision by the referee and was ordered to leave the bench. The referee gave the coach three minutes to leave or the team would forfeit the game. When the coach remained after the three minutes, the referee did indeed declare the game a forfeit and left the court.

"This takes me back 25 years," Naismith told the *Kansas City Star*. "We used to have a lot of excitement like this in the old days. I remember an official who used to work a lot of our games, and he positively would not start a contest unless he was certain there was an open window in the dressing room, which might, if necessary, serve as a means for an escape."

Despite the imperfections in the game, including what Naismith saw as teams spending too much time working on drills in practice instead of just playing games, Naismith thought the future of his game looked good. In 1939 the game had never been more popular, and almost every high school and college in the United States had a team. According to estimates, the game was played by 20 million people around the world.

"I am not worried about the future of basketball, because the game itself is interesting no matter how you fool with it," he said. "If a game is interesting it will last, and basketball is just that. . . . It is a good, stable game.

"In the past forty years, we have made wonderful progress in the skills acquired in basketball and there is no reason to anticipate that the limit has been reached or that new skills may not further be introduced. Each coach is devising new plays and new schemes to gain the upper hand in the contest. The dribble has developed from the rolling of the ball on the floor. A number of ways of passing the ball will be devised. The pivot will be perfected to a greater degree and there is good reason to think that new plans will be devised as long as the game is played."

Naismith, while not worried about the game, did express some concerns. "The rules must be kept simple," he said. "If they become too complex, the general public will lose interest." Naismith was also concerned about coaching—not only in basketball, but in all sports. "The trouble with athletes today is that we demand of a coach that he win most of his games or we whop off his head, and this may happen even in the middle of the season," Naismith wrote. "In this way the unscrupulous can be more successful than the honest, and the institution dismisses the honest that they may get one who is not so scrupulous. This happened in Missouri when Haherington insisted that Kansas was using ineligible men and they asked him why he did not use them also. He stood up for the straight and narrow. They relieved him and secured another. The interesting thing is that I knew that he had at least three ineligible men on his baseball team but he would not believe me and insisted that all his men were Simon pure amateurs.

"The coaches can fool the athletic board, the faculty and some of the students but the players know all the underhand measures that are being used and it is not to their benefit."

As he had many years earlier in one of his early philosophical debates with Phog Allen, Naismith emphasized that a coach should possess qualities other than a desire to win at all costs. "When the coaches realize that winning the game is subordinate to the development of their individuals, they will realize their responsibility and endeavor to meet it," Naismith wrote. "When this time comes, I have not a question but that basketball will make forward strides—probably not as extensive as in the past but will be used more and more as a means of developing the individual in the different phases of physical education, especially in the reflex, social and moral attributes."

As pleased as Naismith was about the state of basketball, he was even more excited about his upcoming retirement from the university. He had worked hard all of his life, and he was now looking forward to spending more time with Maude, his children, and his grandchildren.

CHAPTER 14

Death of a Legend

N aismith had been severely disappointed when Maude was unable to accompany him on his trip to Europe and the Olympics, and he was glad to be back home with her. The two really were soul mates, and all of the letters Naismith wrote to her during his extended time away from home testified to his love and devotion.

He also was pleased that enough money was left over from the funds collected to pay for his trip to the Olympics that he was able to pay off the mortgage on the family home at 1708 Mississippi Street. The Naismiths began looking into buying a new home in an area on the west side of the university, known as the West Hills, where they could live out their retirement years.

Naismith turned 75 on November 6, 1936. Along with six other professors, he was eligible to retire from the university by June 1937, becoming a professor emeritus. He would still be working for the university, receiving half of his former salary, but would not have any specific teaching assignments; rather, he was supposed to make himself available to the university to serve in different ways.

For Naismith, that mostly meant traveling around the state and the country making speeches and appearances at a variety of meetings and functions, although he did not always have the university in mind when it came to choosing the topic of his speeches. Never shy about expressing an opinion on an issue, Naismith carried that philosophy into retirement.

One activity that Naismith's children thought might be good for him was to write a book about his life and about basketball. Once again, however, the timing was unkind to Naismith.

After struggling with the project, Naismith enlisted the help of his son Jack. They spent months together writing and rewriting, and even asked an English professor to offer assistance. Before they could finish the final draft and submit *Basketball* to a publisher, they found out they had not completed the book quickly enough.

Once again, Naismith had lost a race with Phog Allen when he didn't even know he was in a competition. Allen, it turned out, had been writing his own book, and he finished his *Better Basketball* more quickly. The Naismiths did not know about Allen's book until a copy was left inside their screen door one morning.

Naismith realized that much of his book contained the same information as Allen's, and he knew a publisher would not be interested in old material. Naismith's book would eventually be published, but not until 1941, two years after his death.

The book might have finally allowed Naismith to make some money from his invention of the game. Even though he never worried about capitalizing on his invention, others thought it wrong that he was so quick to shrug off financial offers that would have made him a rich man. He never took out a patent on the game, and when a lawyer one time suggested that he could be paid a percentage for every ticket sold to every basketball game, he quickly shooed the man out of his office.

With his popularity at an all-time high when he returned from the Olympics, Naismith received a variety of endorsement offers. At the urging of Allen, he did endorse a basketball made by Rawlings and received royalty payments for several years, but that was the only money he ever earned that was directly related to his invention of the game.

One offer he declined came from a tobacco company, and over the years the offer has been reported to have been worth anywhere from $75,000 to $500,000. Naismith was not impressed by the offer because he knew that cigarettes were a health danger, and he would not endorse a product he opposed for any amount of money. Always a man of strong opinions and convictions, Naismith was not about to alter that stance simply to receive a paycheck.

As James and Maude Naismith planned their retirement, they fell in love with a house that had formerly belonged to Frank Strong, the chancellor of the university. Before they could move in, however, tragedy struck. On the night of March 4, 1937, Maude Naismith died in her sleep, apparently from a heart attack.

The couple had been married for 43 years, and his wife's death was a stunning blow for Naismith. He wept privately and mourned in secret, but all of the plans that had been made for his retirement years were now gone. His children and grandchildren tried to comfort him, and he enjoyed their company, but nothing could replace the loss of his beloved Maude.

"There's nothing to do," he said months later to a friend. "I stay at home and read or stare at myself in a glass. I go out and shop or talk with friends. But I can't forget my wife."

One activity that Naismith had always pursued was traveling, and that continued even after Maude's death. His trouble with cars continued, however, and his children always worried when Naismith took off on a trip by himself. His son Jack reluctantly loaned him a car for a trip to St. Louis to visit his daughter Hellen and grandchildren, but when two weeks passed and no one had heard from Naismith, the family became worried. Finally Jack received a postcard from his father, saying he had decided to keep going past St. Louis and had ended up in New York.

Without telling anyone, he then decided to continue his trip into Canada. When at last he returned home to Lawrence, two fenders on the car were badly damaged. Naismith did not divulge what had happened, merely telling his son, "A couple of taps with a hammer will take care of them."

The family was more relaxed when they knew Naismith had a traveling companion, and one such person was Duke D'Ambra, who had become close friends with Naismith despite their age difference of about 30 years. D'Ambra had been teaching at Kansas when he first met Naismith, and he later resigned to become a full-time commercial photographer. Because he worked for himself, he was able to travel whenever Naismith wanted a companion.

After Maude's death, D'Ambra agreed to go with Naismith on a trip that took them 5,000 miles across the country and into Canada. D'Ambra became Naismith's personal public relations man on the trip, often telephoning the sports editor of a newspaper in a town they were about to visit to arrange for a reporter to interview Naismith when they arrived. Naismith enjoyed meeting and talking with people, reminiscing about how he had come to invent the game, and offering his opinions on the game as it was then being played.

After more than a month, the two men returned to Lawrence, without having suffered any serious automobile mishaps. Their biggest accident had come while visiting some of Naismith's relatives on their farm in Canada. Spending the day fishing from a boat on a lake, Naismith fell overboard. D'Ambra panicked, but Naismith kept calm and, despite being almost 76 years old and weighted down with wet clothes and heavy shoes, swam back to the boat and scrambled onboard. D'Ambra still had not calmed down when Naismith told him, "You know I'm a good swimmer. There wasn't anything to worry about. Stop shaking."

While they were in Canada, Naismith had a chance to visit with his childhood friend, Tait McKenzie, and also met with Dr. Allen Dafoe, the physician for the Dionne quintuplets, who had been born three years earlier. "Naismith and D'Ambra saw the quintuplets just as any other visitor does, thru a glass window," the *Lawrence Daily Journal-World* reported. "The little girls, they were amazed to find, have chestnut colored hair instead of black hair. Dr. Dafoe reported that the increasing number of tourists is a problem and at the peak of the summer he estimated that about 5,000 persons would see the girls each day. The roads leading to the nursery are lined with cabins and concessions and in spite of this there is not room to accommodate all the visitors, the men report."

That trip provided the last opportunity for Naismith to meet with Tait McKenzie, who died several months later, on April 28, 1938. His death was a shock for Naismith and caused him a great deal of sorrow.

Another trip Naismith took was back to Montreal to receive an honorary Doctor of Divinity degree from McGill University's Presbyterian College, his alma mater. Such occasions were happy times, but his days were mostly filled by thoughts of his deceased wife.

About the only joy in Naismith's life was provided by his children and grandchildren. For Mother's Day 1938, he wrote a letter addressed "To the Mothers of the Naismith Tribe":

> Greetings from Great Granddad:
>
> Peggy is responsible for my new title and I am proud of it. I only wish that Mother could have seen the boys and known about them even though it would have been impossible for her to recognize the sobriquet of Great Grandmother. There are so many mothers in our tribe that I have to resort to the carbon copy routine.
>
> Let me tell you how proud I am of you mothers and how much I appreciate the hardships that you have willingly endured for the sakes of your children. In this age personal gratification seems to be first and I rejoice that

my children have been willing to forgo many of the selfish pleasures that you might raise up a generation of sound, healthy children.

You cannot know how proud I am of my children, grandchildren and great grandchildren, yes even to the third generation. It makes me feel like a patriarch who has a clan around him. I look into the face of Mother Maude and realize what she did to bring up our family, and realize that each of you have done the same for your dear ones. My heart is filled with love for all the mothers of the clan. My desire is that each of you may have as much pleasure from your children as we have had from ours.

Mother's day comes but once a year but I assure you that for the husbands of you mothers every day is Mother's day. It gives me a great deal of satisfaction that each of you chose a partner whose aim in life is to be the kind of partner that will make your life one of happiness. Just to think that every one of your grandchildren and children have love and affection from and for your mothers and fathers.

With wishes for many years of happiness and success in the lives of your children I am always, Your Dad.

Naismith also used the occasion to write a poem, entitled "Our Mother."

Our Mother; thy halo on Earth has been stolen
By her who will flatter and shirk
But on Earth as in Heaven the crown will be given
To all those who suffer and work.

"Our Mother; No more will we, Honor, delay
To the heart that so loyal and brave
But now will say, and to Earth's latest day
You're the grandest thing God ever gave.

Our Mother; the sweetness of incense surrounds
Each place when thy presence is near
And music abounds in marvelous sounds
That thrill when thy footsteps we hear.

Our Mother; thy hopes and ambitions and fears
Were clustered about us so warm
But naught did we care for the anguishing prayer
That was offered to keep us from harm.

Our Mother; the days of thy sorrows are o'er
When our lives have been anchored secure
And the day that we trace beaming forth from thy face
In the whole world there's nothing so pure.

Our Mother; our lives shall be one long acclaim
Of thy power and influence sweet
That kept away from the wiles of the day
All our honors we'll lay at thy feet.

Naismith knew he would never replace the love of his life, his wife Maude, but he was lonely for female companionship. Both his sons Jack and James had been members of the Sigma Phi Epsilon fraternity at Kansas, and Naismith had served as an adviser for the group. He began to spend more time at the house, looking for people to talk with and help, and he developed a relationship with the housemother of the fraternity, a woman named Florence Mae Kincaid.

Mrs. Kincaid was a widow, having been married to a dentist from Beloit, Kansas, who had died four years earlier. She had moved to Lawrence to work as the housemother of the fraternity, and she had heard about Naismith from her son Jack, who was a student at the university. Even though, at 56 years of age, she was 21 years younger than Naismith, he always had kept himself in good physical condition and was able to keep up with a younger woman. As the two began to spend more time together, they found they enjoyed each other's company.

Naismith's daughter Maude Ann, who was living with her husband and father in the new home in West Hills, wrote letters to her sisters telling them about their father's new romance. None of the daughters were pleased, and they tried to discourage Naismith from becoming involved in a new relationship at his age. Naismith would not be denied, however, and was very proud when he announced one day that he and Florence were going to be married.

The first time Naismith had asked Florence, she had turned him down, as she too had never intended to remarry. Naismith was persuasive, however, and she finally agreed. Naismith did tell his fiancée, before the wedding, that it was his intent and wish to be buried next to Maude in the cemetery in Lawrence when he died. Florence agreed, and the issue was never discussed again.

On June 10, 1939, the couple was married in the First Presbyterian Church in Overland Park, Kansas, during a quiet ceremony. Naismith wanted the wedding held somewhere other than Lawrence to try to keep the news from spreading to the public. There were only 13 guests at the ceremony, including just two of Naismith's children, Maude Ann and Jack.

The couple set off on a long honeymoon by car, heading first to Tulsa, Oklahoma, then to California, and finally north to Canada. Naismith had arranged several speaking engagements and visits to fraternities during the trip, combining business with pleasure. One of the highlights of the trip was supposed to be the chance to reunite with his old friend Amos Alonzo Stagg, who had now left the University of Chicago and become the football coach at the University of the Pacific in California despite the fact that he also was 77 years old. Unfortunately, Stagg had some schedule complications when Naismith was traveling through California, and the two were not able to get together. Naismith and his new wife—who never called him by his first name, referring to him instead as "Doctor"—continued into Canada, visiting some of his relatives, and finally reached Winnipeg, where he was a guest of honor at a reunion dinner of the living members of the AAU basketball team whose plane had crashed six years earlier.

The newlyweds returned to Lawrence on September 1 and moved into the home in West Hills. The couple kept busy decorating their home, and Naismith was pleased when both current and former students dropped in for a visit or to seek him out for advice. The couple planned to spend the winter months in St. Petersburg, Florida, and Naismith was trying to line up appearances at fraternities and other speaking engagements to occupy some of his time.

On November 19, Naismith's daughter Maude Ann, her husband Thomas, and their young son Tommy came to Lawrence from their home in Topeka to have Sunday dinner with Naismith and Florence. The dinner discussion centered on athletics and sports injuries, and Naismith recommended that Maude Ann not allow her young son to play football because he thought the sport had become too dangerous.

After dinner, Naismith stood up and said he was going to his den to retrieve some statistics he had compiled about athletic injuries.

He fell back into his chair. Naismith was rushed to Lawrence Memorial Hospital, where doctors said he had suffered a cerebral hemorrhage. His condition was listed as critical, and the family gathered at the hospital and waited through the night.

The next morning, Naismith regained consciousness and rallied to the point that the doctors allowed him to return home, where he said Florence could care for him.

Two days later, Florence was rubbing Naismith's back with alcohol when she turned away from him for a moment. When she turned back around, Naismith was unconscious. He had suffered a second stroke.

A doctor was summoned, and he decided Naismith's condition was too critical to attempt to move him to the hospital. He was in and out of consciousness for 24 hours, but was unable to speak coherently and fell into a coma.

Four days later, at 1:50 A.M. on Tuesday, November 28, Naismith died.

CHAPTER 15

• • •

A Great Game

In the foreword to Naismith's book, published in 1941, two years after his death, in conjunction with the fiftieth anniversary of basketball's invention, legendary coach Clair Bee wrote, "The fiftieth anniversary of the invention of basketball finds the game recognized as the world's most popular sport. . . . I challenge anyone to read this book and feel anything but admiration and love for this great and simple character who devoted his life and efforts to education and earned the respect and gratitude of millions of athletes throughout the world. Doctor Naismith merits his place as one of the immortals in American education."

Four hundred and seventy-four words. That was the total length of the original 13 rules created by Naismith for his new game that cold December morning in 1891. From that humble beginning, basketball has grown to its current status—played by millions of people of all ages, men and women, around the world and enjoyed by multiple millions of adoring fans.

While Naismith no doubt would be displeased by some aspects of his sport—mostly on the financial and professional side—he no doubt would be honored and thrilled that his sport has remained so popular and is enjoyed by so many people around the world.

Former Georgetown coach John Thompson once said that he thought basketball had done more to bridge the gap between the races than anything else in society. Current Southern Illinois University coach Chris Lowery noted that the game has been responsible for bringing communities together "and nations that probably didn't even talk [to each other] in his [Naismith's] time period."

According to current Kansas coach Bill Self, Naismith would be proud that "the game of basketball has helped in so many ways our culture, our opportunities. There's been so many positives that have come out of that."

In a column in the *Kansas City Star*, published on November 28, 1998—the anniversary of Naismith's death—during a lockout of National Basketball Association (NBA) players, Joe Posnanski wrote:

> Little did he know that his game would bring hope to kids in the inner city; that children would shoot at driveway backboards across America; that there would be a Michael Jordan; that there would be a Hakeem Olajuwon; that neither of them would play one year because a bunch of greedy millionaires, short and tall, could not agree how to share piles of money that could post up Patrick Ewing. . . .
>
> Inventions almost always get away from their inventors. Albert Einstein always hated the idea that his theories inspired the atomic bomb. Naismith no doubt (and for many of the same reasons) would hate that his game became the NBA. . . .
>
> Even when he was alive, people thought Naismith was naïve about his own game. Even Phog Allen, Naismith's pupil and the father of basketball coaching, thought that. People thought he didn't understand the angles and deviations, surely he didn't understand the box-and-one

defense, and the salary cap, and so they figured that basketball had passed him by.

The game did pass him by. Naismith did not dispute
that. He thought, to his death, that basketball should be
played for fun and exercise, for the thrill of a swish, for the
excitement of a steal, for the joy of a moment. He believed
simply that basketball was a pretty good game for kids to
play and that money and grownups might ruin it. He was
a pretty smart guy.

More than 100 years after Naismith invented the game, kids
don't fall in love with basketball with the idea that they one day
might become millionaires playing in the NBA. They might
dream of one day playing in the Olympics and winning a gold
medal. But they shovel snow off the driveway and shoot baskets
for an hour in the dead of winter for one reason—because the
game is fun.

One of Naismith's unwritten rules for his game was that it
be inexpensive to play, requiring neither a variety of equipment
nor a lot of people. His game consisted of a basket and a ball,
and somebody to try to shoot the ball through the basket. His
sport can be played with one person on a side or five. It can be
played on a blacktop or concrete playground in the inner city or
in elaborate gymnasiums. It is played by youths as young as five
years old and by senior citizens. It is played by people confined
to wheelchairs. No other sport can say that.

Basketball has brought us Michael Jordan, Wilt Chamber-
lain, and Bill Russell. It has given the world Bob Cousy, Oscar
Robertson, and Magic Johnson. Jerry West and Larry Bird are
known around the world for one reason—basketball. Youngsters
today have posters of LeBron James, Tim Duncan, or Steve Nash
taped to their bedroom walls because these are the stars of this
generation.

Even young girls can aspire to become the next Rebecca Lobo
or Lisa Leslie. Women's basketball not only thrives at the high

school and collegiate level, a fact which certainly would please Naismith, but it also has an increasing international presence, including at the Olympics. There is even a successful women's professional league. In many ways, the women's game today is closer to the game Naismith created than the men's game.

Larry Bird still remembers the day in high school in French Lick, Indiana, when he fell in love with basketball. "From that point on, basketball was all I thought about, all I wanted to do," he said in *Drive*, his autobiography. "I couldn't wait for school to let out for the summer so I could play ball. I would play at 6 A.M. before school. I would duck into the gym in between classes to get a few shots up and play again after school into the early hours of the next morning, feeling that sleep was a rude intrusion on my practice time."

Much the same way, at the same time, Earvin "Magic" Johnson was growing up in Lansing, Michigan, falling in love with the same game. "No matter what else I was doing, I always had a basketball in my hand," Johnson wrote in his autobiography, *My Life*. "If I was running an errand for my mother, I'd dribble on the way to the store. Just to make it interesting, I'd alternate right hand and left, block by block.

"I remember waking up when it was still dark outside and wanting to play ball so badly that I'd just lie there, looking out the window, waiting for daybreak. If it was too early to go out to the schoolyard, I'd dribble on the street. I'd run around the parked cars and pretend they were players on the other team. All up and down Middle Street people used to open their windows and yell at me for waking them up. But I couldn't help it. The game was just in me."

When Johnson's Michigan State team met Bird's team from Indiana State in the NCAA championship game in 1979, it became the most watched college basketball game in television history. More than 25 million households in the United States tuned in to see the game, and millions more were watching around the world. When the United States and China met in a first-round game in the 2008 Olympics in Beijing, it was estimated that the audience watching the game around the world on television reached 1 billion people.

The growth and popularity of the game would be all that mattered to Naismith. He wouldn't care that generations of players, and fans, could not identify him as the inventor of the game. He often told audiences, "Don't be afraid to work for humanity and wait for your reward."

Naismith didn't seek personal recognition. He didn't try to make a profit on the game. He kept the original copy of the rules folded in a drawer of his desk until a few years before his death, when he gave it to his son James. Most pleasing to him would be the fact that of his original 13 rules, 10 of them basically remain intact and still form the structure of the game.

He would understand, if not agree with, the fact that other people believe he should have earned more recognition for his invention, and no doubt he would appreciate their efforts on his behalf. He would be pleased, and humbled, by the fact that the Naismith Memorial Basketball Hall of Fame in Springfield, Massachusetts, is named in his honor.

In 1998, as part of the celebration of the hundredth anniversary of Naismith's introducing basketball at the University of Kansas, the playing court at Allen Field House was named the James Naismith Court. Some members of Naismith's family, however, were upset that it had taken the university so long to honor one of its most famous professors—nearly 60 years after his death. The family's disappointment was expressed in a letter that his daughter Hellen Naismith Dodd wrote to Phog Allen in 1948.

"I have been back to Lawrence a number of times in the past five years as all three of my sons have been in school there," Mrs. Dodd wrote. "It's really no pleasure to go back because it only makes me realize how very little the university appreciated what my father did for it in the forty years he spent there.

"As far as I know there isn't even a plaque to show he was ever there. . . . This probably seems a little bitter to you but I'm not bit-

ter. I'm only disappointed that people who have received so many
benefits from basketball can take it so for granted. To be quite
frank I wonder if the name Phog Allen would mean so much to
the country if there had been no game of basketball."

Allen responded with a three-page letter in which he recited
all of his attempts over the years to help Naismith both finan-
cially and with recognition for his accomplishments. "I began
efforts to build a Naismith Field House, but I did not get a hearty
response from university authorities as they had other memorials
in mind at that time," Allen wrote. "They were not against a Naismith Memorial, but since we had built a memorial stadium in
1920, they were not sure that we should attempt another athletic
edifice as a memorial. The field house was voted down. A campa-
nile with carillon and memorial drive around the university campus buildings with vistas was substituted.

"Long before I had a Phog Allen basketball and knowing the
debt that the friends of basketball owed Dr. Naismith, I went to
Doctor and said, 'the game of basketball owes you a great debt of
honor and of compensation. Why don't you have a Naismith basketball, a Naismith goal, and other Naismith game equipment?'

"Dr. Naismith looked at me and laughed heartily when he
said, 'You bloody beggar, you are always thinking about money.'"

Allen later continued, "I do not know that the Naismith family had knowledge of this and the thousands of other instances
wherein I had made sincere efforts in his behalf for his comfort
and for his later years. I would not have said these above things
unless I thought that you, your brothers and sisters lacked some
knowledge of these manifold efforts which I made in his behalf.

"I have always felt deeply that since basketball has been one of
the causes of my earning a livelihood, that I owed basketball and
Dr. Naismith a special debt, and I have always tried to keep that
thought in mind."

The new field house was finally built, and opened in 1955, but
was named Allen Field House. There was very little effort made

to name the building after Naismith, or with a combination linking Naismith's and Allen's names. The street that passes in front of the Field House, however, is known as Naismith Drive.

More than 50 years later, members of the Naismith family believe KU officials do appreciate and recognize Naismith's contributions to the university. "It isn't a secret that my grandfather and Phog Allen had a difference of opinion on many issues," said his granddaughter Hellen Dodd Carpenter. "Despite their differences, however, we know that there was a mutual feeling of respect and admiration for each other. Their disagreements were always over philosophical issues, and were never personal. Both also were extremely loyal and proud of their accomplishments at Kansas. I know my grandfather loved KU, and what he thought was best for the institution was always the foremost thought in his mind. He loved God, his family and KU.

"There is one fact about my grandfather's life that I believe is beyond dispute. There may have been more famous people in the history of sports, such as Babe Ruth and Knute Rockne, but no one person has had more of a direct impact on sports than James Naismith. His invention of basketball impacted millions of individuals and thousands of schools and other organizations and institutions. Nobody in history comes close to having that kind of impact on the sports world."

What would have no doubt made Naismith happiest would be the knowledge that, several decades after his death, everyone associated with basketball had the same morals, values, and appreciation for good sportsmanship that he possessed. He was enough of a realist, however, to know that was unlikely to happen.

The fact that his game has become so popular and successful around the world would have made him smile, especially the fact that it is enjoyed by so many young people. A survey by the Federation of State High School Associations found that, in the 2006–2007 school year, there were more U.S. boys' and girls' high school teams in basketball than in any other sport—a total of more than 35,000 teams, serving more than 1 million male and female students.

Add in the millions of pre–high school youths playing the game in boys' and girls' clubs, at the YMCA and the YWCA, in church leagues, in grade and middle schools, and even in pickup games at the park, and it is easy to see that the game has never been more popular.

The growth of women's basketball has done wonders to advance the athletic achievements of women. Naismith would be pleased that the advancement of the sport has had a great deal to do with reducing gender inequity in sports and has even helped erase some of the discrimination against women in other walks of life, just as the men's game has had a great deal to do with easing racial discrimination.

A crowd of more than 41,000 people filled the Hoosier Dome in Indianapolis to watch the Indiana State High School Championship game in 1990, the largest crowd ever to watch a high school basketball game. The NCAA tournament now ranks as one of the leading events on the yearly sports calendar and draws millions of people to the games, either in person or through television.

Overseas, the game has never been more popular. Starting with eight charter members when it was formed in 1932, the International Basketball Federation has grown to 213 member countries, from Afghanistan to Zimbabwe.

The game of basketball has allowed millions of young people to go to college and get an education when otherwise they never would have been able to pay for it. There are people who owe everything they have in their lives to basketball, and they realize that the game has allowed them to do more things than they ever would have thought possible. They know that without the game they could have ended up on the street, in prison, or dead.

At the one hundredth anniversary dinner honoring Naismith in Springfield, Massachusetts, in 1991, several well-known players came up to members of the Naismith family and thanked them for Naismith's creation. That appreciation, no doubt, would have been meaningful to him.

Yet there are people who look at the details of Naismith's life and, by today's standards, consider that he didn't accomplish much. He held many jobs, but never provided a nice life or financial freedom for his family. He never followed the money or even cared whether he profited from his most famous invention. He measured achievement in other, more personal ways, such as his success in getting his message across to a young player named Johnny Williams.

In 1896, Naismith was in Denver, coaching a YMCA team, and Williams was a team member who constantly was losing his temper. "I watched him come off the floor scowling and belligerent and take his seat on the side lines," Naismith wrote. "It wasn't the first time that Johnny had been banished from the game; in fact, there were few games in which he was able to play the entire time without getting into trouble."

Johnny Williams was "a short, stocky, red-haired Welshman. . . . He was an excellent player, and time after time he would play brilliant ball; but eventually he would lose his temper and be told to leave the floor, many times when he was most needed.

"As I watched Johnny leave the floor in this particular game, I decided that I should talk with him. After the game, I asked him to come into the office. When he entered, he was still resentful toward the circumstances that had caused him to leave the game. He scowled at me, ready to take the reprimand that he expected, but still unwilling to admit that he was wrong."

Naismith told Williams that he was a good player, but that his temper was making him a detriment to his team. He said that for Williams to be successful, not only in basketball but in life, he had to learn to control his feelings. Williams agreed to try.

"A short time later, he found, when a foul was called on him, that self-control paid," Naismith wrote. "He started toward the official to protest; then suddenly he remembered his resolution and trotted away, with his face as red as his hair. The next few plays saw Johnny all over the court; he was offense and defense both, and I knew that through this physical effort he was working off his resentment.

"By the end of the season he had so successfully learned to control his feelings that he was the mainstay of the team; his mates unanimously elected him captain for the following year."

Years later, on a trip to Denver, Naismith and Williams got together for a visit. Williams was then a state legislator, and he asked Naismith if he remembered the day he called Williams into his office. When Naismith said yes, Williams told him that "it had helped him to overcome a fault that would have been a serious drawback throughout his life."

Naismith smiled. His sport, basketball, had accomplished exactly what he had intended. He knew that was the greatest reward he could ever receive.

CHAPTER 16

The Man, More Than Basketball

The news of Naismith's death was broadcast around the world, and tributes began to pour in to Lawrence. Plans were made for his funeral, and his body was returned to the family home, where friends, colleagues, and former students paid their last respects.

Writing in the *Emporia Gazette* the day after Naismith's death, a renowned University of Kansas graduate, journalist William Allen White, wrote, "Here is a man who has done a real service to humanity. . . . What a privilege it must have been, what a satisfaction for him to realize that he had done something worthy, something to make people happy, something really useful in this vale of tears. He had not a high talent, but he used what God gave him and made his life count. That is all any of us can do."

The Kansas governor, Payne H. Ratner, sent a message to the Naismith family: "I feel that the nation owes a great debt of gratitude to Dr. Naismith for what he has done in behalf of the youth of our country. Basketball, the game which he originated and did so much to foster, has developed into such proportions that it has become a molder of youthful characteristics and has furnished an opportunity for physical improvement among both boys and girls of our land."

The KU flag on top of Fraser Hall was lowered to half mast, and the university chancellor, Deane W. Malott, said in a statement that "Many nations of the world will feel the loss of this man, who set high standards of personal clean living and was able to infuse the same standards into the lives of hundreds of young men. His contribution to the athletic world of the game of basketball will leave a mark that even time cannot erase."

Another tribute came from Phog Allen, who said, "The youth of the world has lost a great benefactor in Dr. James Naismith. Eighteen million young men all over the world are playing his game of basketball. Dr. Naismith is directly responsible for all the large field houses, the large auditoria and gymnasia where basketball is played today. Before this game was originated there were few large indoor arenas that were used for any indoor sports.

"Dr. Naismith gave to the youth basketball, a game that takes the youngster from the eighth grade to maturity. I once heard eight nationally known educators speaking from the same platform declare that basketball had all the qualities necessary to teach the educable child: poise, rhythm, grace, coordination, development of skills and the development of physical vigor. The speakers were not competitive coaches nor were they athletes. This game, the only international game that is the product of one man's brain, stamps Dr. Naismith as a great educator, a kindly humanitarian and a practical Christian.

"The youth of the world will arise and call Dr. Naismith blessed."

Other messages of condolences poured in by telegram and telephone to the family from across the United States and Canada. The family heard from Amos Alonzo Stagg, and from the two captains of the teams for the first basketball game ever played in the gym class at the YMCA Training School, T. D. Patton of Toronto, Canada, and Eugene S. Libby of Redlands, California.

Ed Hickey, the basketball coach at Creighton University, probably summed up the thoughts of everyone involved in the sport: "We shall all experience a great loss but will forever be thankful for his promotion and leadership in a great game."

Naismith's funeral was held on Friday, December 1, at the First Presbyterian Church in Lawrence. KU students were on Thanksgiving break, but a large crowd filled the church. "He preferred to do his preaching in active living rather than from the pulpit," the Reverend Theodore H. Aszman said in his eulogy. "His business was to prevent human wreckage rather than wait to patch it up. He built a fence at the top of the cliff so that others might not fall off.

"Building character was basic to Dr. Naismith. He watched the game he invented not as a rabid fan, but as a teacher. He wished to observe the influence of the game on the mind and character of the individual who played it. The testimony to him was to a man, not to an inventor. He truly was one of God's noblemen."

One of Naismith's closest friends was not at his funeral, and many people wondered why until they heard Duke D'Ambra's explanation. When they were traveling together a few years earlier, after the death of Maude Naismith, Naismith made an unusual request of his friend. "If I die before you do, Duke, will you promise not to come to my funeral?" Naismith asked.

When D'Ambra wanted to know why Naismith would make such a request, Naismith said he did not want his friend's final remembrance of him to be looking at his body in a casket. "Memories shouldn't be like that," Naismith said. "You and I should remember each other as we are now, smiling and talking."

Naismith's true memorial is the game he invented, the game of basketball, which has been passed down from generation to generation. From the bare iron hoops nailed to a pole or a tree in a city playground or at a country school to the mammoth multimillion-dollar arenas built for professionals, the game is Naismith's legacy.

"An orphan at nine, a lumber jack at 16, a minister, an MD, a boxer, coach, chaplain, Captain in the military, a professor, and most of all—in his eyes—a husband, father, and family man. His love for his God, his family, his adopted country and the thousands of young people he knew is amazing," said Hellen Dodd Carpenter. "He was always in awe of how the world took his game to heart."

Naismith did, indeed, fulfill the mission he set out to accomplish in his life, to "leave the world a little better than he found it."

Index

Rob Rains is a former National League beat writer for *USA Today's Baseball Weekly* and for three years covered the St. Louis Cardinals for the *St. Louis Globe-Democrat*. He is the author or co-author of biographies or autobiographies of Tony La Russa, Ozzie Smith, Mark McGwire, Jack Buck, Red Schoendienst, and many other sports celebrities.

Hellen Carpenter is the granddaughter of James Naismith. For more than forty years she had in her possession more than 300 documents from Naismith's files that were instrumental in crafting this biography.